Y0-CUY-548

Windows 98: Advanced

Instructor's Edition

COURSE
TECHNOLOGY

Thomson Learning.

Australia • Canada • Mexico • Singapore
Spain • United Kingdom • United States

Windows 98: Advanced

VP and GM of Courseware:	Michael Springer
Series Product Managers:	Caryl Bahner-Guhin, Charles G. Blum, and Adam A. Wilcox
Developmental Editor:	Josh Pincus
Production Editor:	Ellina Beletsky
Project Editor:	Debbie Masi
Key Tester:	Don Tremblay
Series Designer:	Adam A. Wilcox
Cover Designer:	Efrat Reis

COPYRIGHT © 2001 Course Technology, a division of Thomson Learning. Thomson Learning is a trademark used herein under license.

ALL RIGHTS RESERVED. No part of this work may be reproduced, transcribed, or used in any form or by any means—graphic, electronic, or mechanical, including photocopying, recording, taping, Web distribution, or information storage and retrieval systems—without the prior written permission of the publisher.

For more information contact:

Course Technology ILT
One Main Street
Cambridge, MA 02142

Or find us on the Web at: www.course.com

For permission to use material from this text or product, contact us by
• Web: www.thomsonrights.com
• Phone: 1-800-730-2214
• Fax: 1-800-730-2215

Trademarks

Course ILT is a trademark of Course Technology.

Some of the product names and company names used in this book have been used for identification purposes only and may be trademarks or registered trademarks of their respective manufacturers and sellers.

Disclaimer

Course Technology reserves the right to revise this publication and make changes from time to time in its content without notice.

ISBN 0-619-01432-6

Printed in the United States of America

1 2 3 4 5 MZ 04 03 02 01

Contents

Windows 98: Advanced

Introduction

After reading this introduction, you'll know how to:

A Use Course Technology ILT manuals in general.

B Use prerequisites, a target student description, course objectives, and a skills inventory to properly set students' expectations for the course.

C Set up a classroom to teach this course.

D Get support for setting up and teaching this course.

Topic A: About the manual

Course Technology ILT philosophy

Our goal at Course Technology is to make you, the instructor, as successful as possible. To that end, our manuals facilitate students' learning by providing structured interaction with the software itself. While we provide text to help you explain difficult concepts, the hands-on activities are the focus of our courses. Leading the students through these activities will teach the skills and concepts effectively.

We strongly believe in the instructor-led classroom. For many students, having a thinking, feeling instructor in front of them will always be the most comfortable way to learn. Because the students' focus should be on you, our manuals are designed and written to facilitate your interaction with the students, and not to call attention to the manuals themselves.

We believe in the basic approach of setting expectations, then teaching, and providing summary and review afterwards. For this reason, lessons begin with objectives and end with summaries. We also provide overall course objectives and a course summary to provide both an introduction to and closure to the entire course.

Our goal is your success. We encourage your feedback in helping us to continually improve our manuals to meet your needs.

Manual components

The manuals contain these major components:

1 Table of contents
2 Introduction
3 Units
4 Course summary
5 Reference
6 Index

Each element is described below.

Table of contents

The table of contents acts as a learning roadmap for you and the students.

Introduction

The introduction contains information about our training philosophy and our manual components, features, and conventions. It contains target student, prerequisite, objective, and setup information for the specific course. Finally, the introduction contains support information.

Units

Units are the largest structural component of the actual course content. A unit begins with a title page that lists objectives for each major subdivision, or topic, within the unit. Within each topic, conceptual and explanatory information alternates with hands-on activities. Units conclude with a summary comprising one paragraph for each topic, and an independent practice activity that gives students an opportunity to practice the skills they've learned.

The conceptual information takes the form of text paragraphs, exhibits, lists, and tables. The activities are structured in two columns, one telling students what to do, the other providing explanations, descriptions, and graphics. Throughout a unit, instructor notes are found in the left margin.

Course summary

This section provides a text summary of the entire course. It is useful for providing closure at the end of the course. The course summary also indicates the next course in this series, if there is one, and lists additional resources students might find useful as they continue to learn about the software.

Reference

The reference is an at-a-glance job aid summarizing some of the more common features of the software.

Index

You and the students can use the index to quickly find information about a particular feature or concept of the software.

Manual conventions

We've tried to keep the number of elements and the types of formatting to a minimum in the manuals. We think this aids in clarity and makes the manuals more classically elegant looking. But there are some conventions and icons you should know about.

Convention/Icon	Description
Italic text	In conceptual text, indicates a new term or feature.
Bold text	In unit summaries, indicates a key term or concept. In an independent practice activity, indicates an explicit item that is selected, chosen, or typed by students.
`Code font`	Indicates code or syntax.
Instructor notes.	In the left margin, provide tips, hints, and warnings for the instructor.
Select **bold item**	In the left column of hands-on activities, bold sans-serif text indicates an explicit item that is selected, chosen, or typed by students.
Keycaps like ⏎ ENTER	Indicate a key on the keyboard you must press.

Convention/Icon	Description
	Next to an instructor note, indicates a warning for the instructor.
	Next to an instructor note, indicates a tip the instructor can share with students.
	Next to an instructor note, indicates a setup the instructor can use before delivering a step or activity.

⚠ *Warnings prepare instructors for potential classroom management problems.*

TIPS✓ *Tips give extra information the instructor can share with students.*

📦 *Setup instructor notes give a context for instructors to share with students.*

Hands-on activities

The hands-on activities are the most important parts of our manuals. They are divided into two primary columns. The "Here's how" column gives short directions to the students. The "Here's why" column provides explanations, graphics, and clarifications. To the left, instructor notes provide tips, warnings, setups, and other information for only the instructor. Here's a sample:

Do it!

A-1: Activity Title

Here's how	Here's why
1 Open **Sales**	This is an oversimplified sales compensation worksheet. It shows sales totals, commissions, and incentives for five sales reps.
2 Observe the contents of cell F4	F4 ▼ = =E4*C_Rate
	The commission rate formulas use the name "C_Rate" instead of a value for the commission rate.

Take the time to make sure your students understand this worksheet. We'll be here for a while.

Topic B: Setting student expectations

Properly setting students' expectations is essential to your success. This topic will help you do that by providing:

- Prerequisites for this course
- A description of the target student at whom the course is aimed
- A list of the objectives for the course
- A skills assessment for the course

Course prerequisites

Students taking this course should be familiar with personal computers and the use of a keyboard and a mouse. Furthermore, this course assumes that students have completed the following course or have equivalent experience:

- *Windows 98: Module 1*

Target student

Students who want to learn the advanced features of Windows 98 will benefit most from this course. These features include customizing the Windows 98 desktop and creating Web pages with FrontPage Express.

Course objectives

You should share these overall course objectives with your students at the beginning of the day. This will give the students an idea about what to expect, and also will help you identify students who might be misplaced. Students are considered misplaced when they lack the prerequisite knowledge or when they already know most of the subject matter to be covered.

After completing this course, students will know how to:

- Customize the Start menu, taskbar, and folders and set screen saver passwords.
- View file attributes, thumbnails, file extensions, file associations, and hide and protect files and folders.
- Add a new printer, set a default printer, manage print queue, and set printer options.
- Start a program using Run and MS-DOS Prompt, use Disk Cleanup, Scan Disk, Disk Defragmenter, Scheduled Task Wizard, and the Maintenance Wizard to optimize a computer's performance.
- Use Help to troubleshoot problems, view the Getting Started Book and Windows 98 Updates.
- Work with active content, find a person and information by using Internet search tools.
- Create Web pages by using FrontPage Express, filter Internet content, set security levels and create an Internet profile.

Skills inventory

Use the following form to gauge students' skill levels upon entering the class (students have copies in the introductions of their student manuals). For each skill listed, have students rate their familiarity from 1 to 5, with five being the most familiar. Emphasize that this is not a test. Rather, it is intended to provide students with an idea of where they're starting from at the beginning of class. If a student is entirely unfamiliar with all of the skills, he or she might not be ready for the class. A student who seems to understand all of the skills, on the other hand, might need to move on to the next Module in the series.

Skill	1	2	3	4	5
Customize the Start menu, taskbar and folders					
Set screen saver passwords					
View file attributes and thumbnails					
View and modify file associations					
Hide and protect files and folders					
Add a new printer, set a default printer					
Manage print jobs					
Use Run and MS-DOS Prompt to launch a program					
Use Disk Cleanup, ScanDisk, and Disk Defragmenter					
Use Scheduled Task Wizard and Maintenance Wizard to optimize a computer's performance					
Use Help to troubleshoot printer and memory problems and view Windows 98 Updates					
Work with active content					
Find a person and information on the Internet by using Internet search tools					
Create Web pages by using FrontPage Express					
Filter Internet content and set security levels					
Create an Internet profile					

Topic C: Classroom setup

All of our courses assume that each student has a personal computer to use during the class. Our hands-on approach to learning requires that they do. This topic gives information on how to set up the classroom to teach this course. It includes minimum requirements for the students' personal computers, setup information for the first time you teach the class, and setup information for each time that you teach after the first time you set up the classroom.

Student computer requirements

Each student's personal computer should have:

- A keyboard and a mouse.
- A 486DX, 66 MHz or higher processor.
- A minimum of 24 MB RAM.
- Enough hard disk space to install Windows 98, which is typically 210–260 MB.
- A 3.5" floppy disk drive and a 3.5" floppy disk.
- A VGA or higher resolution monitor (Super-VGA is recommended).
- A local printer, named HP LaserJet 4MP, installed on each student's computer.
- Internet access for Units 5 and 6.

First-time setup instructions

The first time you teach this course, you must perform the following steps to set up each student's computer:

1 Install Windows 98, second edition according to the software manufacturer's instructions. This will be a default installation.

2 Install FrontPage Express on each student's computer. Use Windows Update to install FrontPage Express. After connecting to the Windows Update Microsoft site, click on Product Updates. From the available software options, check FrontPage Express and download it. The shortcut to FrontPage Express should appear in the Internet Tools submenu. To open FrontPage Express, the students will have to navigate to Start, Programs, Accessories, Internet Tools, FrontPage Express.

3 If necessary, create Internet accounts for the students. Students will need Internet access to complete Units 5 and 6. E-mail accounts aren't required.

4 Download the StudentData examples for the course. You can download the student data directly to student machines, to a central location on your own network, or to a disk. Please note that for this course the name of the folder that contains the data files is not "Student Data" but "StudentData."

   1 Connect to www.courseilt.com.

   2 Click the download link for Windows 98 Module 2.

   3 Follow the instructions that appear on your screen to save the data files.

Setup instructions for every class

Every time you teach this course, you must perform the following steps to set up each student's computer:

1 If necessary, reset any defaults that were changed in previous classes.

2 Delete the contents of the Student Data folder, if necessary. (If this is the first time you are teaching the course, create a folder called StudentData at the root of the hard drive. Please note that for this course the name of the folder that contains the data files is not "Student Data" but "StudentData.")

3 Copy the data files for the course to the StudentData folder (see the instructions in the preceding section about how to download the data files).

4 A local printer driver for the printer HP LaserJet 4MP needs to be installed on each student's computer before they begin the activities for Unit 3. The idea is to install just the printer driver and not physically install the printer. The driver must be installed before class so that the students are able to install the driver for HP LaserJet 5MP in class without the Windows 98 CD.

Topic D: Support

Your success is our primary concern. If you need help setting up this class or teaching a particular unit, topic, or activity, please don't hesitate to get in touch with us. Please have the name of the course available when you call, and be as specific as possible about the kind of help you need.

Phone support

You can call for support 24 hours a day at (888) 672-7500. If you don't connect to a live operator, you can leave a message, and we pledge to return your call within 24 hours (except on Saturday and Sunday).

Web-based support

The Course ILT Web site provides several Instructor Tools for each course, including course outlines and answers to frequently asked questions. To download these files, go to www.courseilt.com/instructor_tools.html.

Unit 1

Customizing the user interface

Complete this unit, and you'll know how to:

A Customize the Start menu.

B Customize the taskbar.

C Set custom folder options and modify advanced folder settings.

D Protect a computer's resources by setting screen saver passwords.

Topic A: Customizing the Start menu

Explanation

With the many applications on your computer, there are always some applications that you use more frequently than others. You can organize these applications to make them easily accessible from the Start menu. The Start menu can be customized by moving or copying applications into it. You also can add and delete applications to and from the Start menu.

Moving and copying Start menu items

You can move and copy Start menu items by using the shortcut menu. You use the Move Here option to move an item and the Copy Here option to copy an item. It is better to copy an item, than to move it, so that the original menu structure isn't disturbed.

To move or copy a menu item, click Start and navigate to the application you want to move or copy. Right-click the application and drag it to the desired location. When you release the mouse button, a shortcut menu appears. Click Move Here to move the application, and Copy Here to copy the application.

Do it!

A-1: Moving and copying Start menu items

Here's how	Here's why
1 Click **Start**	You'll move a Start menu item to another location.
2 Choose **Programs**, **Accessories**	You'll move an item from this menu to the first level of the Start menu.
3 Right-click and drag **Notepad** from the Accessories menu and drop it above **Windows Update**	

⚠ *Tell students to be sure to drag Notepad onto the Start menu, otherwise they'll create a desktop shortcut.*

A shortcut menu appears when you drop Notepad.

Observe the shortcut menu

> **Move Here**
> Copy Here
> Create Shortcut(s) Here
>
> Cancel

It provides options to move or copy Notepad or to create its shortcut.

4   Choose **Move Here**   To move Notepad to this location. Notice that Notepad is added above Windows Update.

5   Open the Accessories menu   Choose Programs, Accessories.

    Observe the menu   Notepad is no longer present in this menu.

6   Right-click and drag **Paint** from the Accessories menu and drop it above **Notepad**   You'll copy Paint to the first level of the Start menu. Notice that a shortcut menu appears.

7   Choose **Copy Here**   To copy Paint at this location. Notice that Paint is added above Notepad.

8   Open the Accessories menu

    Observe the menu   Paint is still available in the menu.

Adding Start menu items

Explanation   You can add items that you frequently use to the Start menu. You also can delete items that you don't generally use.

To add an item to the Start menu:

1   Choose Start, Settings, Taskbar & Start Menu to open the Taskbar Properties dialog box.
2   Click the Start Menu Programs tab.
3   Under Customize Start menu, click Add.
4   Click Browse.
5   Navigate to the file or application you want to add to the Start menu.
6   Click Next.
7   Select the folder in which you want to place the shortcut.
8   Click Next
9   Click Finish.
10 Click OK.

Do it!   **A-2: Adding Start menu items**

Here's how	Here's why
1 Choose **Start**, **Settings**, **Taskbar & Start Menu...**	To open the Taskbar Properties dialog box. You'll add an item to the Start menu.
2 Click the **Start Menu Programs** tab	To view the options under this tab.
3 Under Customize Start menu, click **Add**	To open the Create Shortcut dialog box.
4 Click **Browse**	(To open the Browse dialog box.) You'll navigate to the application that you want to add to the Start menu.
5 Navigate to **C:\Windows\Notepad**	You'll add Notepad to the Start menu.
Click **Open**	
Click **Next**	To open the Select Program Folder dialog box.
6 From the Select folder to place shortcut in list, select **Accessories**	You'll place the shortcut in the Accessories submenu.
Click **Next**	To open the Select a Title for the Program dialog box.
Observe the Select a name for the shortcut box	It displays the name for the program that will appear in the Start menu.
7 Click **Finish**	To close the dialog box.
8 Click **OK**	To close the Taskbar Properties dialog box.

Deleting Start menu items

Explanation

To delete an item from the Start menu, you can right-click the item and choose Delete from the shortcut menu.

Do it!

A-3:   Deleting Start menu items

Here's how	Here's why
1 Choose **Start**, **Programs**, **Accessories**	Notice that Notepad is added in the Accessories submenu.
Observe the first level of the Start menu	It contains Notepad. You'll delete this item from the Start menu.
2 Right-click **Notepad**	
3 Choose **Delete**	
	The Confirm File Delete message box appears.
4 Click **Yes**	To send the deleted item to the Recycle Bin.
5 Click anywhere on the desktop	To hide the Start menu.

Topic B: Customizing the taskbar

Explanation

To work more efficiently, you can customize the taskbar in a variety of ways. For quick access to your applications, you can add shortcuts to the taskbar. You can further customize the taskbar by adding the Address toolbar and the Links toolbar. With the Address toolbar, you can access the Internet from the taskbar by typing the address of a specific Web site. The Links toolbar consists of quick links that are used to access the Internet without having to type the address of a Web site. By adding a floating toolbar for a folder or a drive, you can access files of that folder or drive from the desktop.

The Quick Launch toolbar

The Quick Launch toolbar is located next to the Start button on the taskbar. The three icons on this toolbar are Show Desktop, Launch Internet Explorer Browser, and Launch Outlook Express. You can launch these applications by clicking the desired icon. You can add applications or documents that you frequently use to the Quick Launch toolbar. For example, if your work involves calculations, you can add the Calculator to the Quick Launch toolbar.

Do it!

B-1:   Adding shortcuts to the Quick Launch toolbar

Here's how	Here's why
1 Observe the Quick launch toolbar	
	You'll add a shortcut to the toolbar.
2 Choose **Start**, **Programs**, **Accessories**	You'll create a shortcut to Calculator on the Quick Launch toolbar.
3 Right-click and drag **Calculator** from the desktop and drop it on the Quick Launch toolbar as shown	
	To add the Calculator to the Quick Launch toolbar.
Choose **Create Shortcut(s) Here**	To create the shortcut.
Observe the Quick Launch toolbar	
	Notice that the Calculator icon appears on the Quick Launch toolbar.

⚠ *Remind students not to drag the shortcut onto existing icons. If they do this, a toolbar will be created instead of a shortcut.*

The Address toolbar

Explanation

If you frequently access the Internet, you can add the Address toolbar to the taskbar. You can use the Address toolbar to type an address and connect to a Web site without opening a browser. Every time you visit a site, the address is automatically stored in the Address toolbar list.

The Address toolbar also can be used to open files and folders. You can open a file by typing its path in the Address toolbar. To add the Address toolbar to the taskbar, right-click the taskbar and choose Toolbars, Address. To remove the Address toolbar, right-click the taskbar and choose Toolbars, Address.

Do it!

B-2:   Adding the Address toolbar to the taskbar

Here's how	Here's why
1 Right-click on a blank area of the taskbar	To open the shortcut menu. You'll add the Address toolbar to the taskbar.
2 Choose **Toolbars, Address**	
Observe the taskbar	The Address toolbar appears on the taskbar.

The Links toolbar

Explanation

The Links toolbar consists of shortcuts to frequently accessed Web sites. These are the same shortcuts that appear in the Links menu in Internet Explorer. When you click a site's shortcut on the Links toolbar, Internet Explorer automatically opens and connects you to the site. You can add the Links toolbar by right-clicking the taskbar and choosing Toolbars, Links. To delete the Links toolbar perform the same steps again. You also can delete the Links toolbar by right-clicking it and choosing Close to open the Confirm Toolbar Close dialog box, and then clicking OK.

Do it!

B-3:   Adding the Links toolbar to the taskbar

Here's how	Here's why
1 Right-click on a blank area of the taskbar	You'll add the Links toolbar to the taskbar.
2 Choose **Toolbars, Links**	
Observe the taskbar	Links 🖉 Best of the Web 🖉 Channel Guide 🖉 Customize Links »
	The Links toolbar appears on the taskbar. Also notice that the Address toolbar is now partially visible.
3 Right-click the **Links** toolbar	You'll remove the Links toolbar from the taskbar.
Choose **Close**	(To close the Links toolbar.) The Confirm Toolbar Close dialog box appears.
Click **OK**	To remove the Links toolbar from the taskbar.

Ensure that students don't right-click on the contents of the Links toolbar.

A floating toolbar

Explanation

You can create a floating toolbar for a drive or folder that you frequently access. By creating a floating toolbar for a folder, you can open it to view its contents directly from the desktop. A floating toolbar can be placed anywhere on the desktop. For example, if you want to open a file on the C: drive, you can open it from the floating toolbar on your desktop. You can create a folder consisting of frequently used applications and create a floating toolbar for that folder. This way you can customize the contents of the floating toolbar to further simplify your access to applications. Any toolbar present on the taskbar can be made into a floating toolbar.

To create a new floating toolbar:

1   Right-click the taskbar.
2   Choose Toolbars, New Toolbar to open the New Toolbar dialog box (as shown in Exhibit 1.1).
3   From the list, select the folder or the drive for which you want to create a toolbar.
4   Click OK to create the toolbar on the taskbar.
5   Drag and drop the toolbar from the taskbar to the desired location on the desktop.

Exhibit 1-1: The New Toolbar dialog box

Do it!

B-4:   Creating a floating toolbar

Here's how	Here's why
1 Open Windows Explorer	Choose Start, Programs, Windows Explorer.
2 Create a folder named **Tools** on the C: drive	Select (C:), right-click on a blank area in the right pane, and choose New, Folder. Then name the new folder Tools.
3 Copy **Notepad** to Tools	Navigate to C:\Windows.
Copy **Wordpad** to Tools	Navigate to C:\Program Files\Accessories.
Copy **Mspaint** to Tools	Navigate to C:\Windows\Start menu\Programs\Accessories.
4 Close Windows Explorer	
5 Right-click on the taskbar	You'll create a floating toolbar for the Tools folder.
6 Choose **Toolbars, New Toolbar...**	To open the New Toolbar dialog box, as shown in Exhibit 1.1.
7 Double-click **(C:)**	

Ensure that students don't right-click any toolbar present on the taskbar.

8   From the list, select **Tools**   The Tools folder is on the C: drive.

9   Click **OK**

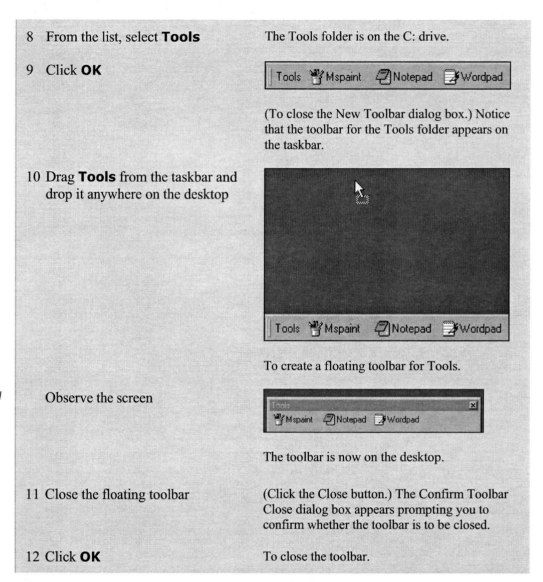

(To close the New Toolbar dialog box.) Notice that the toolbar for the Tools folder appears on the taskbar.

10 Drag **Tools** from the taskbar and drop it anywhere on the desktop

To create a floating toolbar for Tools.

Tell students that this will show the contents of the Tools folder.

Observe the screen

The toolbar is now on the desktop.

11 Close the floating toolbar   (Click the Close button.) The Confirm Toolbar Close dialog box appears prompting you to confirm whether the toolbar is to be closed.

12 Click **OK**   To close the toolbar.

Topic C: Folder options

Explanation

Windows 98 provides various options to customize a folder. You can differentiate a specific folder from others by changing its background color. You also can change advanced settings that are applicable for all folders. For example, you can set an option to display the full path of every folder on the title bar of Windows Explorer and My Computer. Any customization can be reset when necessary.

Customizing a folder

The contents of a folder in Windows Explorer appear with a white background. You can change the appearance of a folder by:

- Changing the background color.
- Setting a graphic image as the background.
- Creating your own Web page and using it as the background.

To set your own Web page as a folder's background, you must use HTML (HyperText Markup Language).

You can use the Customize this Folder Wizard to change the appearance of a folder.

To customize a folder:

1 Choose Start, Programs, Windows Explorer.
2 Select a folder that you want to customize.
3 Choose View, Customize this Folder to start the Customize this Folder Wizard.
4 Select Choose a background picture to set a background for the selected folder.
5 Follow the instructions given by the wizard.
6 Click Finish.

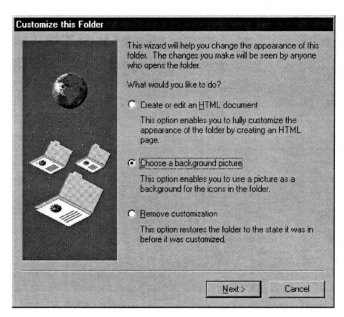

Exhibit 1-2: The Customize this Folder wizard

Do it!

C-1: Setting custom folder options

Here's how	Here's why
1 Choose **Start**, **Programs**, **Windows Explorer**	You'll set custom folder options.
2 From the Folders pane, select **My Documents**	(The My Documents folder is on the C: drive.) You'll customize this folder.
3 Choose **View**, **Customize this Folder...**	To start the Customize this Folder wizard.
4 Select **Choose a background picture**	You'll change the background of the selected folder.
5 Click **Next**	
6 From the Background picture for this folder list, select **BACKGRND.GIF**	Background picture for this folder: [None] 1STBOOT.BMP BACKGRND.GIF Black Thatch.bmp Blue Rivets.bmp Bubbles.bmp Carved Stone.bmp (You'll use this picture as the background for the selected folder.) Notice the preview of this picture in the left pane of the wizard.

7 Click **Next**	A message appears to inform you about the changes you've made to the folder.
8 Click **Finish**	To apply the new background. Notice that the background in the right pane has changed.

Advanced folder settings

Explanation

In addition to customizing a particular folder, you can set advanced options to customize all folders with the same settings. For example, "Display the full path in title bar" and "Hide file extensions for known file types" are some of the advanced folder settings.

To modify advanced folder settings:

1 Open Windows Explorer.
2 Choose View, Folder Options.
3 Click the View tab.
4 Make the necessary changes by selecting or deselecting the required options.
5 Click OK.

Do it!

C-2: Modifying advanced folder settings

Here's how	Here's why
1 Choose **View, Folder Options...**	To open the Folder Options dialog box.
2 Click the **View** tab	You'll change the settings under the View tab.
3 In the Advanced settings list, under Files and Folders, check **Allow all uppercase names** and **Display the full path in title bar**	
4 Click **OK**	To apply the new settings and close the Folder Options dialog box.
5 Observe the title bar	Notice that the full path of the open folder appears on the title bar.
6 Close Windows Explorer	

Topic D: Password-protected screen savers

Explanation

A screen saver is deactivated when you press a key on the keyboard or move the mouse. However, if you are working on confidential data, you might want to assign a password to the screen saver so that it can't be deactivated without entering the password. This protects your computer from unauthorized access or use.

Screen saver passwords

To assign a password to your screen saver:

1 Right-click the desktop.

2 Choose Properties to open the Display Properties dialog box.

3 Click the Screen Saver tab.

4 Under Screen Saver, select the screen saver you want to set.

5 Specify the number of minutes after which the screen saver will appear if there is no mouse or keyboard activity.

6 Check Password protected.

7 Click Change.

8 In the New password box, enter a new password.

9 In the Confirm new password box, enter the same password.

10 Click OK to set the password.

11 Click OK to confirm the change in password.

12 Click OK to close the Display Properties dialog box and apply the settings.

Do it!

D-1: Assigning a password to a screen saver

Here's how	Here's why
1 Right-click anywhere on the desktop	You'll assign a password to a screen saver.
2 Choose **Properties**	To open the Display Properties dialog box.
3 Click the **Screen Saver** tab	To view the items under the Screen Saver tab.
4 Under Screen Saver, from the list, select **Flying Windows**	You'll apply this screen saver.
5 Edit the Wait box to read **2**	To set the time after which the screen saver will appear.

Tell students that the computer has to be idle for the specified time before the screen saver appears.

6	Check **Password protected**	![Screen Saver dialog: Flying Windows selected, Password protected checked, Wait 2 minutes]
		To protect the screen saver by using a password.
7	Click **Change**	(To open the Change Password dialog box.) You'll assign a password.
8	In the New password box, enter **Spices**	This is the password you'll assign to the screen saver.
	In the Confirm new password box, enter **Spices**	To confirm the assigned password.
9	Click **OK**	![Microsoft Windows message box: The password has been successfully changed. OK]
		A message box appears confirming the change in password.
10	Click **OK**	To confirm the change in password.
	Click **Apply**	To apply the settings.
11	Click **Preview**	To test the password protected screen saver.
	Move the mouse	When you move the mouse, the Windows Screen Saver dialog box appears.
	In the Type your screen saver password box, enter **Spices**	To specify the password that will deactivate the screen saver.
	Click **OK**	To access the desktop after deactivating the screen saver.
12	Click **OK**	To close the Display Properties dialog box and apply the settings.

Tell students that the password for the screen saver isn't case sensitive. So they can enter "Spices" or "spices."

Unit Summary: Customizing the user interface

Topic A In this unit, you learned how to **customize the Start menu**. You can customize the Start menu by **moving** and **copying** frequently used applications to the Start menu. You also learned to **add** and **delete** items from the Start menu.

Topic B Next, you learned how to **customize the taskbar** by adding shortcuts to the **Quick Launch toolbar** and adding the **Address and Links toolbars**. You also created a **floating toolbar**.

Topic C Then, you learned how to set **custom folder options** to change the appearance of a folder by choosing a background picture. You also learned how to **modify advanced folder settings** by changing the options in the Folder Options dialog box.

Topic D Finally, you learned how to **assign a password** to a **screen saver**. Screen savers can be protected to avoid unauthorized use of your personal documents.

Independent practice activity

1 Copy **Windows Update** from the Start menu to the **Accessories** submenu.

2 Add **PBRUSH** to the Programs submenu (PBRUSH is in C:\WINDOWS).

3 Delete Windows Update from the Accessories submenu.

4 Add **Notepad** to the Quick Launch toolbar.

5 Remove the **Address toolbar** from the taskbar.

6 Create a floating toolbar for the **StudentData** folder.

7 Close the floating toolbar.

8 Open **Windows Explorer**.

9 Change the background picture of the folder StudentData to **Pinstripe**.

10 Close Windows Explorer.

11 Assign a password **Cloves** to Channel Screen Saver.

Unit 2

Managing files and folders

Complete this unit, and you'll know how to:

A View file attributes, enable thumbnail view, and use file attributes to hide and protect data.

B View file extensions and associations, and modify associations.

Topic A: File and folder attributes

Explanation

Attributes are special properties that you can apply to files and folders. These properties determine whether a file can be modified, it's visible in the folder hierarchy, or can be backed up. By altering a file or folder's attributes, you can ensure a greater level of integrity.

File attributes

Windows 98 provides four types of attributes that can be set for files and folders. The following table describes the attributes.

Attribute	Description
Read-only	A file that has the Read-only attribute can be opened but no permanent changes can be made to its contents. However, a Read-only file can be deleted.
Hidden	A file or folder that has the Hidden attribute can't be viewed in Windows Explorer or My Computer. This prevents others from knowing that the file or folder exists.
Archive	Set by default, a file or folder that has the Archive attribute can be backed up by certain applications.
System	A file that has the System attribute is a special file used by the operating system. This attribute is assigned by the operating system.

To view a file or folder's attributes, right-click the file or folder and choose Properties. The attributes appear in the General tab of the Properties dialog box.

Do it!

A-1: Viewing file attributes

Here's how	Here's why
1 Open Windows Explorer	You'll view the file attributes.
2 From the Folders pane, select **StudentData**	To view the files in StudentData in the right pane.
3 Right-click **Pepper**	In the right pane.
4 Choose **Properties**	To open the Pepper Properties dialog box.
Observe the Attributes	Attributes: ☐ Read-only ☐ Hidden ☑ Archive ☐ System
	Notice the different file attributes.

5	Observe Read-only	(This option is cleared.) If you check this option the file will be available for only reading and not for writing.
6	Observe Hidden	(This option is cleared.) You can check this option to hide the file.
7	Observe Archive	(This option is checked.) If this option is checked, Windows 98 identifies this file as a file to be backed up by certain applications.
8	Observe System	This attribute isn't available. The operating system sets this attribute for certain special files it uses.
9	Click **Cancel**	To close the Pepper Properties dialog box.

Hiding files and folders

Explanation

You can hide files and folders that are confidential. By hiding a file or folder, you can make the file unavailable for others to use. The hidden file or folder can't be accessed if its name and path are unknown.

To hide files and folders:

1 Open the Folder Options dialog box.
2 Right-click the file or folder.
3 Choose Properties.
4 Under Attributes, check Hidden.
5 Click OK.
6 Choose View, Refresh.

Do it!

A-2: Hiding files and folders

Here's how	Here's why
1 Right-click **Spicesdata**	(To open the shortcut menu.) You'll hide this file.
2 Choose **Properties**	To open the Spicesdata Properties dialog box.
3 Under Attributes, check **Hidden**	To hide the file.
Click **OK**	To apply the settings.
4 Choose **View, Refresh**	
Observe the right pane	The file is no longer visible.

Viewing hidden files

Explanation

After hiding a file, you might want to view it again. To view hidden files:

1. Choose View, Folder Options to open the Folder Options dialog box.
2. Click the View tab.
3. Under Files and Folders, check Show all files.
4. Close the Folder Options dialog box.
5. Select the file.
6. Choose File, Properties to open the file's Properties dialog box.
7. Under Attributes, clear Hidden.
8. Close the file's Properties dialog box.

Do it!

A-3: Viewing hidden files

Here's how	Here's why
1 Choose **View, Folder Options...**	(To open the Folder Options dialog box.) You'll view all of the files including the hidden ones.
2 Click the **View** tab	To view the View tab options.
3 Under Files and Folders, observe the various options	Notice that Do not show hidden or system files is selected.
4 Under Files and Folders, select **Show all files**	By checking this option you'll be able to view all of the files including the hidden files.
5 Click **OK**	To apply the settings and close the Folder Options dialog box.
6 Observe Spicesdata	It is now visible in the folder hierarchy but its icon is shaded.
7 Open the Spicesdata Properties dialog box	You'll clear the Hidden attribute that you set for this file.
Under Attributes, clear **Hidden**	To make the file visible in the folder hierarchy.
Click **OK**	To apply the settings and to close the Spicesdata Properties dialog box.
Choose **View, Refresh**	
Observe Spicesdata	It is now visible in the folder hierarchy similar all of the other files.

Protecting files and folders

Explanation

If you want to protect files and folders without hiding them, you can assign a Read-only attribute. In this case, your protected file can be opened, but no permanent changes can be made to it. Even if somebody tampers with your file by making changes in its content, the person will not be able to save the file with those changes.

To make a file or a folder Read-only:

1 Right-click the file or folder.
2 Choose Properties.
3 Select the General tab.
4 Under Attributes, check Read-only.
5 Click OK.

Do it!

A-4:   Protecting files and folders

Here's how	Here's why
1 Right-click **Clovesdata**	(To view the shortcut menu.) You'll apply the Read-only attribute to this file.
2 Choose **Properties**	
3 Under Attributes, check **Read-only**	 Attributes: ☑ Read-only ☐ Hidden ☑ Archive ☐ System To make the file Read-only.
Click **OK**	To close the dialog box and apply the Read-only attribute to the file.
4 Open Clovesdata	Double-click to open it.
5 Delete **Cloves**	The heading of the document.
6 Choose **File**, **Save**	The Save As dialog box appears.
7 Click **Save**	Save As ⚠ C:\StudentData\Clovesdata.txt This file exists with Read Only attributes. Please use a different file name. [OK] The Save As message box appears indicating that the file exists with a Read Only attribute.
Click **OK**	To close the message box.

8 Close the Save As dialog box	
9 Close Clovesdata	A message box appears to confirm whether you want to save the changes.
Click **No**	To close the message box.

Thumbnails

Explanation

A thumbnail is a small preview of a file's contents. You can use thumbnail view when you want to collectively view the contents of all of the files in a folder. Although you can use thumbnail view for all file types, it is more useful for graphic files and HTML (Web) pages. It also can be used to preview sound and video files. You can open a file by double-clicking the preview of the file. Thumbnails can be set in Windows Explorer or My Computer.

To view thumbnails:

1   Open Windows Explorer.
2   In the right pane, right-click the folder that you want to see in thumbnail view.
3   Choose Properties to open the Folder Properties dialog box.
4   Check Enable thumbnail view.
5   Click OK.
6   Double-click the folder containing image files.
7   Choose View, Thumbnails.

Do it!

A-5: Viewing thumbnails

Here's how	Here's why
1 In the Folders pane, select **(C:)**	To view the contents of the C: drive in the right pane.
2 In the right pane, right-click **StudentData**	To open the shortcut menu.
3 Choose **Properties**	To open the StudentData Properties dialog box.
4 Check **Enable thumbnail view**	To enable thumbnail view for the folder.
5 Click **OK**	To close the dialog box.
6 Double-click **StudentData**	To view the contents of this folder in the right pane.
7 Choose **View, Thumbnails**	To view the thumbnail preview of the files.
Observe the right pane	Notice that the preview of the image file appears.
8 Choose **View, List**	To view the contents in the folder in List format.

Topic B: File associations

*Explanation*A *file association* is the mechanism that you use to open a file in the appropriate application by simply double-clicking it. You can do this because Windows 98 uses file extensions to associate each file with a particular application.

File extensions

File extensions refer to the characters that are appended to the end of file names. Specifically, file extensions are the characters that appear to the right of the "dot" (.) in a file name. All files have extensions. When you save a file in an application, Windows 98 appends the extension that corresponds with that application. Windows 98 "knows" what application a file is associated with by what type of file extension it has. The following table lists some common file extensions and the applications with which they are associated.

File type	Extension	Associated application
Text document	txt	Notepad
Bitmap image	bmp	Paint
Document	doc	WordPad

To view file extensions:
1 Choose View, Folder Options to open the Folder Options dialog box.
2 Click the View tab.
3 From the Advanced settings list, under Files and Folders, clear Hide file extensions for known file types.
4 Click OK.

Do it!

B-1: Viewing file extensions

Here's how	Here's why
1 Choose **View, Folder Options...**	To open the Folder Options dialog box.
2 Click the **View** tab	To see the View tab options.
3 From the Advanced settings list, under Files and Folders, clear **Hide file extensions for known file types**	
	To view the file extensions for the known file types.
4 Click **OK**	To confirm the changes.
Observe the file names	You'll see that the file extensions are now visible.

Working with file associations

Explanation

You can view how file associations function by opening files that have different file extensions. You'll observe that different file extensions are related to different applications. It is essential to understand how file associations function, so that by looking at the file extension you can deduce what application it is associated with. For example, a file that has a .txt extension will always open in Notepad, and a file that has a .bmp extension will always open in Paint.

Do it!

B-2:   Working with file associations

Here's how	Here's why
1 Observe the file extension of Spicesdata.txt	Notice that it's .txt. You'll now see the application associated with this file.
2 Double-click **Spicesdata.txt**	The file opens in Notepad.
3 Close Notepad	Choose File, Exit.
4 Observe the file extension in Pepper.bmp	Notice that it's .bmp.
5 Open Pepper.bmp	The file opens in Paint.
Close Paint	

Tell students that they will be observing different file extensions associated with different applications.

Modifying file associations

Explanation

In some cases, you can change the application with which a file is associated. For example, you might want to view text (.txt) files in WordPad. By default, text files open in Notepad. By altering the file associations for files with .txt extensions, you can tell Windows 98 to open text files in WordPad. Exercise caution when changing file associations. For example, Windows 98 will alter a file association so that you can open a WordPad document in Notepad. However, when you actually open the file, it will be illegible.

Do it!

B-3:   Modifying file associations

Here's how	Here's why
1 Choose **View**, **Folder Options...**	To open the Folder Options dialog box.
2 Click the **File Types** tab	To view the File Types tab options.
3 From the Registered file types list, select **Text Document**	

Registered file types:
- Snapshot File
- SpeedDial
- Streaming Audio / Video file
- Streaming Audio / Video shortcut
- Task Scheduler Queue Object
- Task Scheduler Task Object
- Text Document
- TIF Image Document
- TrueType Font file

(You'll have to scroll down the list.) You'll change the file association for text documents.

Here's how	Here's why
4 Click **Edit**	To open the Edit File Type dialog box.
Click **Edit**	To open the Editing action for type: Text Document dialog box.
5 Click **Browse**	(To open the Open With dialog box.) You'll navigate to the application you want to associate the action with.
6 Navigate to **C:\Program Files\Accessories**	
Select **WORDPAD.EXE**	This is the application you'll associate the action with.
Click **Open**	
7 Click **OK**	(To close the Editing action for type: Text document dialog box.) To confirm the change in settings.
Click **Close**	To close the Edit File Type dialog box.
8 Click **Close**	To close the Folder Options dialog box.
9 Open Spicesdata.txt	The text document opens in WordPad.
10 Close WordPad	

Unit Summary: Managing files and folders

Topic A   In this unit you learned how to view **file attributes** and **thumbnails**. File attributes are special properties of files and folders. The four types of file attributes are Read-only, Hidden, Archive, and System. You also learned how to use thumbnails for graphic files. Finally, you learned how to **hide** and **protect** data. You can hide a file or folder by checking the Hidden attribute for that file or folder. You can protect a file by converting it to Read-only.

Topic B   Then, you learned how to view **file extensions**, view **file associations** in action, and modify file associations to open a file in a different application.

Independent practice activity

1   View the attributes of the **StudentData** folder.

2   Enable Thumbnail view for the **StudentData** folder. Change the View settings to **List**.

3   Hide the file extensions for known file types.

4   Modify the file association of all text files to open in **Notepad**. (*Hint:* NOTEPAD is in C:\WINDOWS.)

5   Clear the option to show all files in Windows Explorer. (Use the View tab in the Folder Options dialog box.)

6   Set the **Archive** attribute for the StudentData folder.

Unit 3

Print management

Complete this unit, and you'll know how to:

A Add a new printer and set a default printer.

B Print documents, manage the print queue, and set printer options.

Topic A: Printer setup

Explanation

Before you can print a document, you need to set up a printer. In Windows 98, a *printer* is the software your computer uses to communicate with a physical printing device. Each physical printing device has its own software, called a *printer driver*. To print to a particular physical printing device, you must install the appropriate printer driver. You can install a local printer or a network printer provided you have the printer driver. A driver is a hardware device or program that controls or regulates another device. There are two types of drivers, the Line driver and the Device driver. Device drivers are used for connecting printers.

You can use Windows 98 to install local and network printers. A local printer is a physical printing device attached directly to your computer. A network printer is shared with other network users. Typically, system administrators install and share network printers.

Adding a new printer

You use the Add Printer Wizard to install both local and network printers. To install either type of printer, you must have access to the appropriate printer driver. All of the printer drivers that come bundled with Windows 98 are available on the Windows 98 CD. However, various printer drivers might also be installed on your hard drive. In this case, you don't need the CD to install or re-install a printer driver.

To add a new printer:

1 Choose Start, Settings, Printers.
2 Double-click Add Printer to start the Add Printer Wizard.
3 Click Next.
4 Select either a Local printer or a Network printer.
5 Click Next.
6 Follow the instructions given by the wizard.

Do it!

A-1: Adding a new printer

Here's how	Here's why
1 Choose **Start, Settings, Printers**	(To open the Printers window.) You'll add a new printer. Notice that a local printer already is installed.
2 Double-click **Add Printer**	To start the Add Printer Wizard.
3 Click **Next**	To begin installing your printer.
4 Verify that **Local printer** is selected	You'll install a local printer on the computer.
Click **Next**	To continue the printer installation.

5　From the Manufacturers list, select **HP**

(You'll need to scroll down the list.) You'll install an HP printer.

From the Printers list, select **HP LaserJet 5MP**

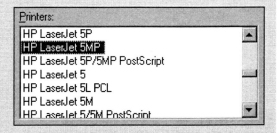

Click **Next**

6　Under Available ports, verify that **LPT1: Printer Port** is selected

To specify the printer port.

Click **Next**

To continue with the installation.

7　Observe the Printer name box

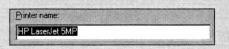

Notice that the name of the printer you are adding appears.

Under Do you want your Windows-based programs to use this printer as the default printer, verify that **No** is selected

Don't set this printer as the default printer.

Click **Next**

8　Select **No**

You won't print a test page.

Click **Finish**

Observe the Printers window

Notice that the HP LaserJet 5MP icon appears.

Setting a default printer

Explanation

In Windows 98, if there are one or more printers installed, one of them must be set as the default printer. If only one printer is installed on your computer it is automatically set as the default printer. All of the print jobs that you send to the printer are automatically transferred to the default printer, unless otherwise specified. You can change the default printer as often as you want.

In some programs, such as Notepad, you can't choose the printer from which you want to print. These programs print directly to the default printer. If there are many printers installed on your computer, it's convenient to set the printer that is closest to your workstation as the default printer.

Do it!

A-2: Setting a default printer

Here's how	Here's why
1 Observe the Printers window	The HP LaserJet 4MP includes a check mark, indicating that it's set as the default printer.
2 Right-click **HP LaserJet 5MP**	(To open the shortcut menu.) You'll set this as the default printer.
3 Choose **Set as Default**	To set this as the default printer.
Observe the printer icon	A check mark now appears above the HP LaserJet 5MP printer icon, indicating that it's the default printer. A check mark no longer appears above the HP LaserJet 4MP printer.

⚠ *These icons will only appear when the Large icons option is selected in the View menu.*

Topic B: Managing print jobs

Explanation

After you add a printer to your computer, you can print documents. Part of learning how to print effectively is learning how to manage the print queue and set printer options.

Printing documents

You can send documents to a printer by opening Windows Explorer, selecting the document you want to print, and choosing File, Print. This sends all of the document pages to the default printer.

You also can print a file by first opening it in its associated application, and then choosing File, Print. This opens the Print dialog box in which you can set options for printing, such as the number of copies required and the pages to be printed.

Do it!

B-1: Pausing the printer and printing documents

Here's how	Here's why
1 Right-click **HP LaserJet 5MP**	
Choose **Pause Printing**	To temporarily halt all of the print jobs issued to the printer.
2 Open Windows Explorer	You'll send a file to be printed.
3 Navigate to **C:\StudentData**	You'll print files present in this folder.
4 Select **Spices**	
5 Choose **File**, **Print**	(To print the document.) Notice that the file opens in the associated application and the Printing message box appears indicating the progress of printing. The message box closes after all of the document pages have been sent for printing, and then the application closes.
6 Select **Cloves**	
7 Choose **File**, **Print**	
8 Close Windows Explorer	

Managing the print queue

Explanation

When you send multiple documents to a printer, the printer keeps track of the documents in the *print queue*. You can see all of the print jobs in the print queue by double-clicking the printer. The print queue displays the information listed in the following table.

Item	Description
Document Name	Displays the file being printed and the source program of the file.
Status	Displays the status of the print job as printing, paused, or cancelled.
Owner	Displays the name of the person who sent the print job.
Progress	Displays the size of the print job and how much of it has printed.
Started At	Displays the time and date on which the print job was issued.

When working on a network, it's important to manage your print jobs. Managing your print jobs consists of viewing the print queue, pausing the printing of a document, and deleting the printing of a document. To manage your print jobs in the print queue, double-click the printer containing your document.

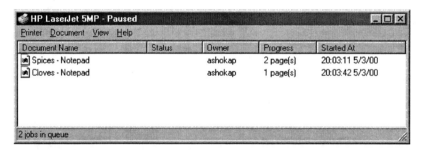

Exhibit 3-1: A paused print queue

Do it!

B-2:   Managing the print queue

Here's how	Here's why
1 Double-click **HP LaserJet 5MP**	To view the print queue.
Observe the various column headings	You'll see the details of the document in the print queue.
2 Select **Spices**	You'll pause the printing of Spices.
3 Choose **Document, Pause Printing**	To pause the printing of Spices.
Observe the Status column	It indicates that the Spices print job is paused.
4 Choose **Document, Pause Printing**	To resume the printing of the document.
5 Select **Cloves**	To remove Cloves from the print queue.
Choose **Document, Cancel Printing**	
Observe the Document Name column	Notice that the print job for this file is no longer present in the print queue.
6 Select **Spices**	You'll cancel the printing of this document.
7 Choose **Document, Cancel Printing**	To cancel printing of Spices.
8 Close the printer window	

Tell students that pausing the printer will pause all of the print jobs. However, they also can pause a specific print job.

Setting printer options

Explanation

Windows 98 provides a number of printer options that you can set to customize your print jobs. You use the Properties dialog box to set printer options. To open the Properties dialog box, right-click the printer and choose Properties. The properties dialog box is composed of seven tabs you can use to set printer options. The following table lists and describes each of the tabs.

Tab	Function
General	This tab is used to specify a comment about the printer for network users to view and to print a test page.
Details	This tab is used to add and delete printer ports and specify the printer drivers to be used.
Sharing	This tab is used to share the printer to users on a network.
Paper	This tab is used to set the size of the paper on which you want to print. You also can set the option of printing the document in portrait or landscape orientation. There are different paper sizes available, such as letter, legal, and executive.
Graphics	This tab is used to select the type of graphics, the print resolution, and *dithering*. In a monochrome printer, the dithering option can be used to create an illusion of varying shades of gray to make an image more attractive. In a color printer, dithering treats the different areas of an image as groups of dots that are colored in different patterns
Fonts	This tab is used to set the cartridges to be used for printing and to manage printer fonts.
Device Options	This tab is used to set the print quality and printer memory

To set Printer options:
1   Choose Start, Settings, Printers.
2   Right-click the printer for which you want to set printer options.
3   Choose Properties.
4   Click the Paper tab.
5   Select the paper size you want.
6   Click the Graphics tab.
7   Select the desired resolution.
8   Under Dithering, select a dithering type.
9   Click the Device Options tab.
10 From the Print quality list, select the desired quality.
11 Click OK.

Do it!   **B-3:   Setting printer options**

Here's how	Here's why
1 Right-click **HP LaserJet5MP**	You'll set the printer properties.
Choose **Properties**	(To open the printer's Properties dialog box.) The General tab is selected by default.
2 Click the **Paper** tab	You'll specify the paper size.
3 Select **A4**	
4 Click the **Graphics** tab	You'll specify the nature of the graphics.
5 From the Resolution list, select **300 dots per inch**	
6 Under Dithering, select **Fine**	
7 Click the **Device Options** tab	
8 From the Print quality list, select **RET -Medium**	To specify the quality of text that you'll use for your printouts.
9 Click **OK**	To apply the settings and to close the Properties dialog box.
10 Close the Printers window	

Unit Summary: Print management

Topic A In this unit, you learned how to **add a printer** to your computer. You also learned how to set a **default printer**.

Topic B Finally, you learned how to **manage the print queue** and set printer options.

Independent practice activity

1 Add a printer named **HP LaserJet 4** as a local printer. Set it as the default printer.

2 Pause the printer.

3 Print **C:\StudentData\Company memo**.

4 Print **C:\StudentData\Cardamom**.

5 Pause the printing of **Cardamom**.

6 Delete **Company memo** and **Cardamom**.

7 Change the printing paper size to **Legal**. Change the resolution to **150 dots per inch**. Set dithering to **None**.

8 Close all open windows.

Unit 4

System utilities

Complete this unit, and you'll know how to:

A Use Run and MS-DOS Prompt to start a program.

B Use Disk Cleanup, Scan Disk, and Disk Defragmenter.

C Use the Scheduled Task Wizard and the Maintenance Wizard to optimize your computer's performance.

Topic A: The Run command and the MS-DOS Prompt

Explanation

You usually use the Start menu to start applications. However, to start applications that don't appear on the Start menu, or that have been deleted from the Start menu, Windows 98 provides the Run command and the MS-DOS Prompt features. To use these features, you need to know the application's name that you want to start. Note, that the name you enter in Run or from the MS-DOS Prompt is often different from the name that you select from the Start menu. For example, to run Windows Explorer by using the Run command, you enter the name "explorer."

The Run command

You can use the Run command to open any application, folder, file, or Internet site. To use the Run command, choose Start, Run, and enter the name of the application in the Run dialog box. The Run dialog box provides a Browse button to help you find the application you want to run.

Do it!

A-1: Using Run to start a program

Here's how	Here's why
1 Choose **Start, Run...**	(To open the Run dialog box.) You'll start Windows Explorer using the Run dialog box.
2 Click **Browse**	To open the Browse window.
3 Navigate to **C:\Windows\Explorer**	You'll start Windows Explorer.
Click **Open**	
Observe the Run dialog box	Notice that the path of the application appears.
4 Click **OK**	To close the Run dialog box and open Windows Explorer.
5 Close Windows Explorer	

The MS-DOS Prompt

Explanation

You can use the MS-DOS Prompt to use Windows 98 as though it were MS-DOS. This is useful when you are running old MS-DOS applications that can't use the Windows 98 graphical user interface. To open the MS-DOS Prompt window, choose Start, MS-DOS Prompt. An MS-DOS command window opens and places you in the C:\Windows directory by default. You can use MS-DOS commands to start programs and move around in a directory hierarchy. Unlike the Run command, there is no Browse button to assist you in navigating the directory hierarchy.

Do it!

A-2:   Using MS-DOS Prompt to start a program

Here's how	Here's why
1 Choose **Start**, **Programs**, **MS-DOS Prompt**	(To open the MS-DOS Prompt window.) You'll start Windows Explorer by using the MS-DOS Prompt window.
Observe the window	
	You can type commands here to start the associated application.
2 Type **explorer**	This is the name of the application you want to start.
3 Press (↵ ENTER)	To open Windows Explorer.
Observe the screen	The Windows Explorer window appears.
4 Close Windows Explorer	
5 Type **exit**	
Press (↵ ENTER)	To close the MS-DOS Prompt window.

Topic B: Disk utilities

Explanation

Among the worst problems you can encounter when using your computer are problems with your hard disk. Windows 98 provides several disk utilities to help you keep your hard disk in good working order.

Disk Cleanup

Over a period of time, your hard disk becomes filled with files that you no longer need. This is especially true if you frequently use the Internet. Knowing that it's impossible for users to delete all unwanted files manually, Windows 98 provides the Disk Cleanup utility. Running the Disk Cleanup utility deletes the files listed below.

- Temporary Internet Files: When you visit Web sites, the information on the pages you visit is stored on your computer as temporary files. After a couple of days, these temporary files might consume a lot of hard disk space.

- Offline Web Pages: If you visit a Web site in offline mode, all of the pages of that Web site are saved on your computer.

- Downloaded Program Files: Often when you visit Web sites, the files necessary to view the site are downloaded to your computer. Although these files are necessary while you are viewing the site, after leaving the site they are no longer necessary.

- Recycle Bin: Until the Recycle Bin is emptied, the files that have been moved there still occupy disk space.

- Temporary Files: When you run programs on your computer, some temporary files are stored in C:\Windows\Temp. Usually these files are automatically deleted when a program closes.

When you run the Disk Cleanup utility, it first displays the amount of hard disk space that is being utilized by each of the above file types. Disk Cleanup provides you with the option to select the type of files you want to delete. To run Disk Cleanup, choose Start, Programs, Accessories, System Tools, Disk Cleanup.

Do it!

B-1:   Using Disk Cleanup

Here's how	Here's why
1 Choose **Start**, **Programs** **Accessories**, **System Tools**, **Disk Cleanup**	You'll use Disk Cleanup.
2 In the Drives list, verify that **(C:)** is selected	You'll use Disk Cleanup to delete unwanted files from the hard disk.
Click **OK**	(A progress bar appears that calculates the amount of disk space you can recover after you perform Disk Cleanup.) To open the Disk Cleanup for (C:) dialog box.
3 Verify that the **Disk Cleanup** tab is active	
4 Under Files to delete, check **Temporary Internet Files**, **Downloaded Program Files**, and **Temporary files**	Files to delete: ☑ Temporary Internet Files 3.37 MB ☐ Offline Web Pages 0.00 MB ☑ Downloaded Program Files 0.00 MB ☐ Recycle Bin 12.09 MB ☑ Temporary files 12.25 MB
Click **OK**	To delete Temporary Internet Files, Downloaded Program Files, and Temporary files. The Disk Cleanup for (C:) message box appears.
Click **Yes**	To confirm the deletion and start the cleanup process.

Tell students that the Offline Web Pages option might not be available in the list on their computer if they haven't saved any offline Web pages.

Tell students that the size of the files might differ.

ScanDisk

Explanation

You can use the ScanDisk utility to detect and fix errors related to the hard disk and memory. The files in your computer are internally stored in *clusters*. A cluster is a disk storage unit that further consists of *sectors*. Sectors are used by the operating system to read or write information. A single file can be stored in several clusters. At times there can be errors in the sectors of the hard disk. Such errors can be detected and fixed by ScanDisk. You can use ScanDisk to perform two types of tests:

- Standard test can be used to check files and folders for errors.
- Thorough test can be used to check files and folders for errors as well as scan disk surface for errors.

To run ScanDisk, choose Start, Programs, Accessories, System Tools, ScanDisk.

Do it!

B-2: Using ScanDisk

Here's how	Here's why
1 Choose **Start**, **Programs**, **Accessories**, **System Tools**, **ScanDisk**	You'll use ScanDisk to find errors on the hard disk.
2 Verify that **(C:)** is selected	![ScanDisk - [C:] Select the drive(s) you want to check for errors: 3½ Floppy (A:) [C:]]
	To specify that you want to check the C: drive for errors.
3 Under Type of test, verify that **Standard** is selected	To check files and folders for errors.
4 Check **Automatically fix errors**	To automatically fix the detected errors.
5 Click **Start**	To start scanning.
Observe the ScanDisk dialog box	Notice the progress bar while the disk is being scanned. When the process is complete, the ScanDisk Results message box appears.
Observe the ScanDisk Results message box	ScanDisk Results - [C:] ScanDisk did not find any errors on this drive. 1,079,836,672 bytes total disk space 0 bytes in bad sectors 16,023,552 bytes in 487 folders 16,842,752 bytes in 224 hidden files 839,942,144 bytes in 7,911 user files 207,028,224 bytes available on disk 32,768 bytes in each allocation unit 32,954 total allocation units on disk 6,318 available allocation units [Close]
	It displays the statistics for the hard disk.
6 Click **Close**	To close the message box.
7 Click **Close**	To close the ScanDisk dialog box.

The Disk Defragmenter

Explanation

When you save a file to the hard disk, the operating system locates some free disk space and stores it. When the operating system doesn't find enough disk space to accommodate the entire file in a single area of the hard disk, it stores the file in fragments. You don't realize this when you run an application or open a file due to the speed of your computer. When the amount of data you have stored in your computer is very large and is divided into several small fragments, it takes more time to open the files. To avoid this problem, use Disk Defragmenter to reorganize the fragments. Disk Defragmenter stores the file or application as a complete unit on a single area of the disk. The process of reorganizing the fragments into one unit is known as defragmenting.

To start the Disk Defragmenter, choose, Start, Programs, Accessories, System Tools, Disk Defragmenter.

Do it!

B-3:   Using Disk Defragmenter

⚠ *Tell students that it might take a long time to complete the defragmenting process.*

Here's how	Here's why
1 Choose **Start**, **Programs**, **Accessories**, **System Tools**, **Disk Defragmenter**	(To open the Select Drive dialog box.) You'll defragment the hard disk.
2 In the Which drive do you want to defragment list, verify that **Drive C Physical drive** is selected	
3 Click **OK**	To begin defragmenting.
Observe the screen	
	The progress bar indicates the progress of defragmenting.
4 Click **Show Details**	To open the Defragmenting window.
Observe the window	There are multiple colored boxes with each box representing one disk cluster. During the process, you'll notice that the colors of different boxes change.

Tell students that they might have to a while to view these boxes.

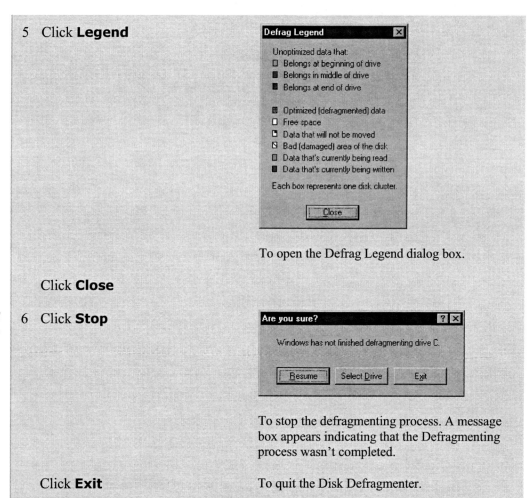

5   Click **Legend**

To open the Defrag Legend dialog box.

Click **Close**

Tell students that they will
not wait for the process to
be completed as it might
take a lot of time.

6   Click **Stop**

To stop the defragmenting process. A message box appears indicating that the Defragmenting process wasn't completed.

Click **Exit**

To quit the Disk Defragmenter.

Topic C: Optimizing system performance

Explanation

Regularly using system utilities such as ScanDisk and Disk Defragmenter can help you optimize the performance of your computer. However, ScanDisk and Disk Defragmenter take a long time to run. You can use the Scheduled Task Wizard and the Maintenance Wizard to run these time-consuming activities during non-work hours.

The Scheduled Task Wizard

You can schedule a list of tasks to be performed by the operating system by using the Scheduled Task Wizard. For example, you can schedule the Disk Defragmenter to run at night when you aren't using your computer. You also can schedule it to run on a monthly basis depending on your needs. However, your computer has to be turned on at the scheduled time for the task.

To use the Scheduled Task Wizard to schedule tasks, choose Start, Programs, Accessories, System Tools, Scheduled Tasks.

Do it!

C-1:   Using the Scheduled Task Wizard

Here's how	Here's why
1 Choose **Start, Programs, Accessories, System Tools, Scheduled Tasks**	To open the Scheduled Tasks window. You'll use the Scheduled Task Wizard to schedule tasks, such as defragmenting and scanning your hard disk.
2 Double-click **Add Scheduled Task**	To start the Scheduled Task Wizard.
3 Click **Next**	You'll select the task to be scheduled.
4 From the list, select **Disk Defragmenter**	(Scroll down if necessary.) To choose Disk Defragmenter as the task to be scheduled.
5 Click **Next**	The Wizard screen indicates that you can give the task a new name and specify how often you want to perform the task.
6 Select **One time only**	To perform the task once every week.
7 Click **Next**	

Depending on how quickly you perform the steps, you might have to adjust the start time by a minute or two.

8 Edit the Start time to **3** minutes from the current time

Start time:

5:30 AM

To start the Disk Defragmenter 3 minutes from now.

9 Click **Next**

Observe the wizard screen

The task has been successfully scheduled. The Wizard displays the date and time when this task will be performed.

10 Click **Finish**

To finish the scheduling of tasks. The Disk Defragmenter icon appears.

11 Wait for the Disk Defragmenter to start

12 Exit the Disk Defragmenter

Click Stop to Exit.

13 Right-click **Disk Defragmenter**

You'll delete this task from the schedule.

Choose **Delete**

Click **Yes**

14 Close the Scheduled Tasks window

The Maintenance Wizard

Explanation

The Maintenance Wizard performs almost the same functions that the Task Scheduler does. The difference is that the Task Scheduler schedules one task at a time and the Maintenance Wizard can collectively perform a range of maintenance activities. The two types of maintenance activities that you can schedule are, Express and Custom. To use the most common maintenance settings, use Express maintenance. To select the maintenance settings, use the Custom maintenance. By using Express maintenance you can make the most frequently used programs run faster, rectify errors on the hard disk, and recover free space on the hard disk without individually scheduling these activities.

To run the Maintenance Wizard choose, Start, Programs, Accessories, System Tools, Maintenance Wizard.

Do it!

C-2:   Running the Maintenance Wizard

Here's how	Here's why
1 Choose **Start**, **Programs**, **Accessories**, **System Tools**, **Maintenance Wizard**	To start the Maintenance Wizard.
2 From the What do you want to do list, select **Custom – Select each maintenance setting myself.**	What do you want to do? ○ Express - Use the most common maintenance settings. ◉ Custom - Select each maintenance setting myself To set a customized maintenance schedule.
3 Click **Next**	
4 From When do you want Windows to run maintenance tasks, select **Custom – Use current settings**	When do you want Windows to run maintenance tasks? ○ Nights - Midnight to 3:00 AM ○ Days - Noon to 3:00 PM ○ Evenings - 8:00 PM to 11:00 PM ◉ Custom - Use current settings To specify the time for running maintenance tasks.
5 Click **Next**	
6 Select **No do not defragment my disk**	◉ No, do not defragment my disk. You won't set a schedule for the Disk Defragmenter.
7 Click **Settings**	To open the settings dialog box.
8 Verify that **(C:)** is selected	You'll scan the hard disk.
Under Type of Test, verify that **Standard** is selected	You'll schedule ScanDisk to perform a Standard test.
Check **Automatically fix errors**	To automatically fix the errors that ScanDisk detects.
Click **OK**	To apply the settings and close the dialog box.
9 Click **Reschedule**	To reschedule this task.
10 From the Schedule Task list, select **Once**	Schedule Task: Once ▼ To perform this task once.

	11 From the Run on list, select the current date and month	(If necessary.) To start ScanDisk on the current day.
Depending on how quickly you perform the steps, you might have to adjust the start time by a minute or two.	12 Edit the Start time box to read 5 minutes from the current time	To run ScanDisk after 5 minutes.
	Click **OK**	
	Click **Next**	
	13 Select **No, do not delete unnecessary files**	You won't set a schedule for Disk Cleanup.
	Click **Next**	Notice that the tasks you scheduled are listed.
Tell students to wait for ScanDisk to start.	Click **Finish**	

Unit Summary: System utilities

Topic A

In this unit, you learned how to start a program using **Run** and **MS-DOS Prompt**. You can use these utilities when the program you want to run doesn't appear on the Start menu.

Topic B

Next, you learned how to delete unimportant files and recover hard disk space by using **Disk Cleanup**, **ScanDisk**, and **Disk Defragmenter**. You learned how to clean up the hard disk by using Disk Cleanup and detect and rectify hard disk errors by using ScanDisk. You also learned how to improve the speed of your computer by using Disk Defragmenter.

Topic C

Finally, you used the **Scheduled Task Wizard** and the **Maintenance Wizard** to schedule tasks to be performed automatically.

Independent practice activity

1   Open **Notepad** by using the Run command.

2   Open **Notepad** by using MS-DOS Prompt.

3   Clean the contents of the **C drive** using Disk Cleanup utility. Close the Notepad window and exit MS-DOS Prompt.

4   Rectify the errors in the **C: drive** by using ScanDisk.

5   Use the Scheduled Task Wizard to schedule Disk Cleanup **weekly** at **8:30 AM** on **Tuesdays** and **Fridays**.

6   Use the Maintenance Wizard to schedule Express maintenance from **Midnight to 3:00 A.M.** (*Hint:* Change the maintenance settings.)

Unit 5

Help and the Windows Update utility

Complete this unit, and you'll know how to:

A Use Help to troubleshoot printer and memory problems, and view the Getting Started Book.

B Use Windows Update to view Windows 98 updates.

Topic A: Using Help

Explanation

Windows 98 provides many advanced Help features to help you find solutions to problems. *Troubleshooters* help you automate the activity of diagnosing and solving problems. Windows 98 also provides an online book, called the *Getting Started Book*, to assist you in working with Windows 98.

Another useful feature of Windows 98 is the Windows Update utility. This utility helps keep your software updated with the latest products offered by Microsoft.

Windows 98 Troubleshooters

The Windows 98 Troubleshooters can be thought of as wizards that guide you through the troubleshooting process. The troubleshooters are organized by topic, making it easy to quickly see whether you can get help for a particular problem. To use the troubleshooters, choose Start, Help and click the Contents tab. Select Troubleshooting and then select Windows 98 Troubleshooters. From the list of topics, select the topic that applies to your particular problem.

Do it!

A-1: Troubleshooting print and memory problems

Here's how	Here's why
1 Choose **Start**, **Help**	(To open Windows Help.) You'll troubleshoot printer problems.
2 Verify that the **Contents** tab is active	To view the Contents tab options.
3 From the left pane, select **Troubleshooting**	To list the troubleshooting topics.
4 Select **Windows 98 Troubleshooters**	To list the Windows 98 troubleshooters.
5 Select **Print**	Windows 98 Troubleshooters ? Networking ? Modem ? Startup and Shutdown ? Print ? DriveSpace 3 ? Memory To display the Windows 98 Print Troubleshooter in the right pane.
Maximize the window	
6 Select **Printing is unusually slow**	

7	Click **Next**	Scroll down in the right pane.
	Observe the right pane	The print troubleshooter suggests that there might be a problem with the print queue. In addition, it offers potential solutions and asks you if any of its prescribed solutions solved the problem.
8	Select **Yes**	

> Try printing your document again. Did this action solve the problem?
> ⊙ Yes.
> ○ No.
> ○ I'd like to skip this step and try something else.

(Scroll down the list in the right pane.) To confirm that your problem has been solved.

9	Click **Next**	

> **Thank you for using the Print troubleshooter.**

A message appears as shown.

10	From the left pane, select **Memory**	To start the Memory troubleshooter.
11	Select **I frequently receive a Parity error message on a blue screen**	
12	Click **Next**	To view the solutions for the problem.
13	Select **No**	You'll need to scroll down.
	Click **Next**	Notice that the troubleshooter has other solutions to your problem.
14	Select **Yes**	
15	Click **Next**	A thank you message appears.

The Getting Started Book

Explanation

The Getting Started Book is an online book that you can read and reference like an ordinary book. Unlike an ordinary book, however, the online book contains *links* that can quickly provide you with related information. A link is text or a graphic that quickly connects the active page to another page. Links are usually differentiated by underlining and coloring. A link changes to a hand when you place the insertion point on it.

To view the Getting Started Book:

1 Click the Contents tab.

2 Select Getting Started Book: Online Version.

3 Select Microsoft Windows 98 Getting Started Book.

4 Click Click here to open the book.

Do it!

A-2: Viewing the Getting Started Book

Here's how	Here's why
1 Verify that the **Contents** tab is active	You'll view the Getting Started Book.
2 From the left pane, select **Getting Started Book: Online Version**	(You'll need to scroll up.) To view the contents in it.
3 Click **Microsoft Windows 98 Getting Started Book**	To view the contents of the Getting Started Book.
Observe the right pane	
	It displays the introduction to the Getting Started Book.
4 Click **Click here**	To open the Getting Started Book.
5 Click **Installing Windows 98**	You'll view information about Installing Windows 98.
6 Under Installing Windows 98, select **Before You Begin**	To view the information on requirements before beginning to install Windows 98.
7 Click **Using Your Desktop**	
8 Click **What Is the Desktop?**	
Maximize the **Getting Started** window	
9 Observe the right pane	It consists of information about desktop. Notice that some words are colored and underlined. These words are links to other pages.

10 In the right pane, click **desktop** as shown

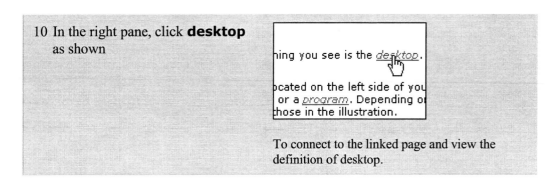

To connect to the linked page and view the definition of desktop.

Searching the Getting Started Book

Explanation

The Getting Started Book is a helpful feature of Windows 98. It is a more elaborate version of Windows Help. In addition to textual information it has tables, screen shots, and graphics. The Getting Started Book also has a search utility that is similar to that of Windows Help.

Do it!

A-3:   Searching the Getting Started Book

Here's how	Here's why
1 Click the **Search** tab	You'll use the Search tab to find information about a topic.
2 Under Type in the keyword to find box, enter **desktop**	
Click **List Topics**	Notice that all of the related topics appear in the left pane, under the Select Topic to display list.
3 Under Select Topic to display, select **Taskbar and Start Button**	(Scroll down the list.) You'll search for information on this topic.
Click **Display**	To display information on the taskbar and Start button in the right pane.
Close the Getting Started Book window	
Close the Help window	

Topic B: The Windows Update utility

Explanation

Windows Update is an online product catalog you can use to upgrade your Windows 98 operating system. By using Windows Update, you can download service packs, system files, and device drivers.

Windows Update

To access the Microsoft Windows Update Web site, choose Start, Windows Update. The Microsoft Windows Update Web site is divided into two panes. The left pane consists of the following links:

- Product Updates: You can use this link to view and install the latest updates for your computer.

- Support Information: This site consists of Frequently Asked Questions and Known Issues pages. There are other support options that also are available.

- Microsoft Windows Family: This site consists of information on the various operating systems provided by Microsoft. You'll also find information on Windows Technologies such as Internet Explorer and Windows Media. There also are links to technical support sites for software developers.

- Microsoft Office Update: You can download all critical updates for your computer from Product Updates. But each Office product has its own catalog of downloads. You can download software from the catalog.

When you click an item in the left pane, the details of that selection are displayed in the right pane.

You can view Windows 98 updates to get information about upgrading your computer's Microsoft software. You can upgrade by downloading the latest updates of software that Microsoft has introduced. To view the required updates, click PRODUCT UPDATES and wait for the Microsoft server to configure your computer. After the server suggests the appropriate updates, check the updates you want to download, and then click the Download button.

Do it!

B-1: Viewing Windows Update

Here's how	Here's why
⚠ *Ensure that an Internet connection is provided before students perform this activity.*	

Here's how	Here's why
1 Choose **Start**, **Windows Update**	To open the Microsoft Windows Update Web site.
2 Click **about Windows Update**	(This button is in the top-right corner of the window.) To view information on Windows Update.
Observe the window

Back to Windows Update

? **About Windows Update**

Windows Update is an online extension of Windows. Currently, Windows Update consists of two areas: the Product Updates catalog and the Support Information area. Use the navigation bar on the left side of your screen to browse these areas.

Contents
About Product Updates
• How does it work?
• What do I need to do?
• Updating device drivers
About Support Information
For corporate IT managers only

It displays information on About Windows Update and provides a list of subtopics on which you can view help. |
3 Under Contents, click **How does it work?**	
Observe the page	You'll see information on how Windows Updates works.
4 Close the active window	
5 Click **Product Updates** as shown	**PRODUCT UPDATES**
Go here to download and install the latest updates for your computer.

To view the updates that are required for your computer. |
Tell students to click Yes if a security message box appears. 6 Observe the window	Notice that Windows Update is configuring your computer to determine the necessary updates.
7 Observe the window	(Scroll down if necessary.) All of the updates your computer needs are stated.
8 Check **Internet Explorer Help**	(Scroll down if necessary.) You'll see how you can download this updated version of Internet Explorer Help.

9 Click as shown	

> ngertips. NOTE: This is
> b. Re̶a̶d this first

	To open the linked Web page that contains information on how to install and uninstall Internet Explorer Help.
10 Close the window	
11 Click **Download**	To download the updated version of Internet Explorer Help.
Observe the window	It asks you for confirmation to install the software and shows the installation steps.
12 Click **Back**	(You'll need to scroll down.) To return to the list of available software. You won't download any software.

Using Support Information

Explanation   Support Information is a list of frequently asked questions. By clicking on a link you get a list of frequently asked questions and their answers. You also have a link to Known Issues on this Web page.

Do it!   **B-2:   Using Support Information**

Here's how	**Here's why**
1 Click **Support Information**	You'll view the support information that is available.
2 Click **Frequently Asked Questions**	To view a list of frequently asked questions and their answers.
3 Click **Known Issues**	(Scroll up the page.) To open the Known Issues – Microsoft Internet Explorer window.
Observe the window	A list of information on known issues appears.
4 Close the Known Issues – Microsoft Internet Explorer window	
5 Close the Microsoft Windows Update – Microsoft Internet Explorer window	

Unit Summary: Help and the Windows Update utility

Topic A

In this unit, you learned how to use the **Windows 98 troubleshooters** to help you troubleshoot printer and memory problems. You also used the **Getting Started Book** to search for help.

Topic B

Finally, you learned how to use the **Windows Update** utility to update your operating system by downloading the updates that your computer requires. You also learned how to use Support Information to view information on frequently asked questions.

Independent practice activity

1 Use the Windows 98 Troubleshooter to remove the new icon that appears on your taskbar. (*Hint:* This is a display problem.)

2 Use the Getting Started Book to view information on **Using Your Desktop**.

3 Search information on **Choosing a Desktop Style** from within the Getting Started Book by using the keyword **Desktop**.

4 Use Windows Updates to see the list of recommended updates.

Unit 6

Working on the Internet

Complete this unit, and you'll know how to:

A Add active content to the desktop, set a custom update schedule, and delete active content.

B Find a person, and work with Internet search tools.

Topic A: Working with active content

Explanation
In addition to providing access to the Internet, Windows 98 provides the *Active Desktop* feature. You can use the Active Desktop to display a Web page on your desktop without opening your Web browser. This is especially useful for Internet content that often changes and that you frequently access, such as news headlines or weather reports. A Web page that is displayed on your desktop is called *active content*.

Adding active content to the desktop

Active content is Internet information that changes at regular intervals on your computer's desktop. In other words, after you add active content to the desktop, the information is updated as it occurs. Active content can be available offline. After adding active content, you don't need to be connected to the site.

To add active content:

1 Right-click the desktop.
2 Choose Active Desktop, Customize my Desktop to open the Display properties dialog box.
3 Click New.
4 Click No.
5 In the Location box, enter the address of a site to add active content from it.

Do it!

A-1: Adding active content to the desktop

Here's how	Here's why
1 Right-click the desktop	
2 Choose **Active Desktop, Customize my Desktop...**	To open the Display Properties dialog box.
3 Click the **Web** tab	If necessary.
4 Check **View my Active Desktop as a web page**	
5 Click **New**	
	To open the New Active Desktop Item dialog box.

6	Click **No**		You'll add active content without using the Active Desktop Gallery.

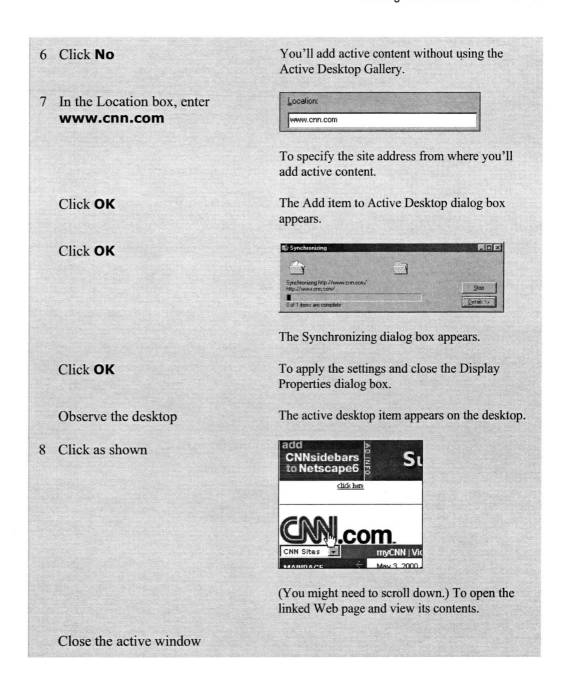

7	In the Location box, enter **www.cnn.com**	
		To specify the site address from where you'll add active content.
	Click **OK**	The Add item to Active Desktop dialog box appears.
	Click **OK**	
		The Synchronizing dialog box appears.
	Click **OK**	To apply the settings and close the Display Properties dialog box.
	Observe the desktop	The active desktop item appears on the desktop.
8	Click as shown	
		(You might need to scroll down.) To open the linked Web page and view its contents.
	Close the active window	

Tell students that a synchronization error might occur.

Using the Active Desktop gallery

Explanation

You also can access Microsoft Active Desktop gallery to add active content. The Active Desktop gallery consists of various topics related to the availability of active content.

To add active content to the desktop:

1 Right-click the desktop.
2 Choose Active Desktop, Customize my Desktop to open the Display Properties dialog box.
3 Verify that the Web tab is active.
4 Check View my Active Desktop as a web page.
5 Click New to open the New Active Desktop Item dialog box.

6 Click Yes to connect to the Desktop gallery.

7 Select the topic for which you need active content on the desktop.

8 Select the content of the topic you want to add to the desktop.

9 Click Add to Active Desktop.

10 Click Yes to confirm.

11 Click OK to add the content.

Do it!

A-2: Using the Active Desktop gallery

Here's how	Here's why
1 Right-click the desktop	You'll add active content to the desktop.
2 Choose **Active Desktop, Customize my Desktop...**	To open the Display Properties dialog box
3 Verify that the **Web** tab is active	To view the contents of the Web tab.
Verify that **View my Active Desktop as a web page** is checked	To view the desktop as a Web page.
4 Click **New**	To open the New Active Desktop Item dialog box.
5 Click **Yes**	To close the dialog box and to connect to the Desktop gallery.
Maximize the window	If necessary.
6 Click **news** as shown	You'll add the News headlines as the active content to your desktop.
7 Click **CNET**	
8 Click **Add to Active Desktop** as shown	(To add the News Headlines as the active content to your desktop.) A message box appears.

Tell students to close the Security Warning message box if it appears.

Observe the message box

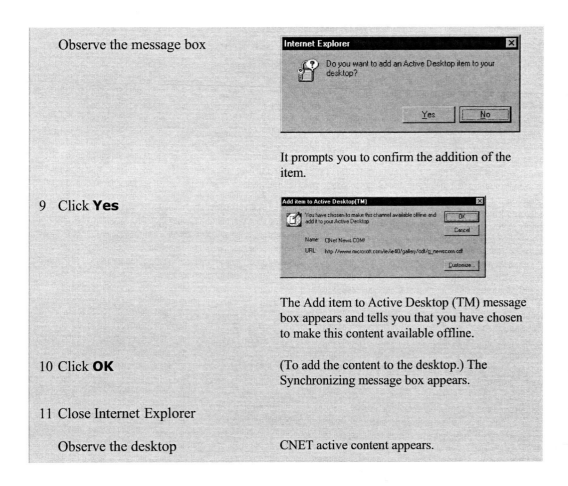

It prompts you to confirm the addition of the item.

9 Click **Yes**

The Add item to Active Desktop (TM) message box appears and tells you that you have chosen to make this content available offline.

10 Click **OK**

(To add the content to the desktop.) The Synchronizing message box appears.

11 Close Internet Explorer

Observe the desktop

CNET active content appears.

Setting a custom update schedule

Explanation

You can set a custom update schedule for your active content. By setting a custom update schedule, you set the exact time and day of the updates.

To set an update schedule:

1 Right-click the desktop.
2 Choose Active Desktop, Customize my Desktop to open the Display Properties dialog box.
3 Click the Web tab, if necessary.
4 Check the active content for which you want to set a custom update.
5 Click Properties.
6 Click the Schedule tab.
7 Click Add.
8 Make necessary changes in the New Schedule dialog box.
9 Click OK to close the New Schedule dialog box.
10 Click OK to close the Properties dialog box.
11 Click OK to close the Display Properties dialog box.

Do it!

A-3: Setting a custom update schedule

Here's how	Here's why
1 Right-click the desktop	You'll set a custom update schedule for the active content you added.
2 Choose **Active Desktop**, **Customize my Desktop...**	To open the Display Properties dialog box.
3 Verify that the **Web** tab is active	
4 Select **CNet News.COM!**	(If necessary.) You'll set a custom update schedule for it.
5 Click **Properties**	To open the CNet News.COM! Properties dialog box.
6 Click the **Schedule** tab	To view the Schedule tab options (as shown in Exhibit 6.1).
Verify that **Using the following schedule(s)** is selected	
7 Click **Add**	To open the New Schedule dialog box.

Tell students that the contents of the days at box will depend on the current date and time.

Observe the dialog box

New Schedule	? X

Please specify settings for your new schedule.

E̲very [1] days a̲t [3:47 AM]

N̲ame: [My Scheduled Update]

☐ If my computer is not connected when this scheduled synchronization begins, automatically connect for me

[OK] [Cancel]

8 In the Every box, verify that **1** is selected	To update the content everyday.
9 Edit the days at box to read **5:00 PM**	To update the content as 5:00 PM everyday.
10 Check the check box as shown	☑ If my computer is not connected when this scheduled synchronization begins, automatically connect for me
	To automatically connect to the Internet for updating the active content if you're not connected at that time.

11 Click **OK**	To close the New Schedule dialog box.
12 Click **OK**	To apply the settings and to close the CNet News.COM! dialog box.
13 Click **OK**	To close the Display Properties dialog box.

Deleting active content

Explanation

You might not want to have the active content permanently on your desktop. You can delete the active content when you don't need it.

To delete active content:

1 Right-click the desktop to open the Display Properties dialog box.
2 Choose Properties.
3 Select the active content that you want to delete.
4 Click Delete.
5 Click Yes to confirm the deletion.

Do it!

A-4: Deleting active content from the desktop

Here's how	Here's why
1 Right-click the desktop	(To open the shortcut menu.) You'll delete the added active content from the desktop.
2 Choose **Properties**	To open the Display Properties dialog box.
Click the **Web** tab	
3 Select **C Net News.COM!**	
4 Click **Delete**	The Active Desktop Item message box appears.
5 Click **Yes**	To confirm the deletion of the active content.
6 Delete **CNN.com**	Select CNN.com and click Delete.
7 Clear **View my Active Desktop as a web page**	
8 Click **OK**	To close the Display Properties dialog box.
Click **No**	You won't view the desktop as a Web page.
Observe the desktop	The active content is no longer present on the desktop.

Topic B: Finding information

Explanation

Although the Internet has information on virtually every subject, finding the information you need isn't always easy. Both Windows 98 and Internet Explorer provide tools to assist you in searching for what you need.

Finding people

You can use the Windows 98 Find tool to search for people on the Internet. Windows 98 can search for people by name or e-mail address. Windows 98 can search your e-mail address book as well as a *directory service*. A directory service provides an electronic directory of people who have Internet access and have registered with a directory service. If you search for a person by name, you'll get information on all of the registered people with that name. If the person that you are trying to find hasn't registered with the directory service you're searching, you won't be able to find information on that person.

To find a person:

1 Choose Start, Find, People.
2 From the Look in list, select Address Book or a directory service.
3 Enter the name in the Name box.
4 Enter the e-mail address in the E-mail box.
5 Click Find Now.

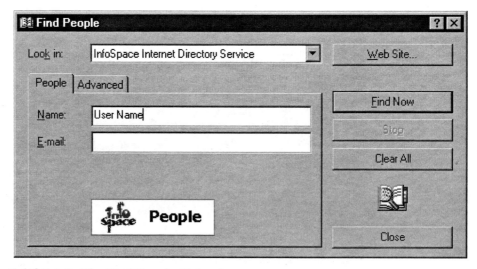

Exhibit 6-1: The Find People dialog box

Do it!

B-1: Finding a person

Here's how	Here's why
1 Choose **Start**, **Find**, **People...**	To open the Find People dialog box. You'll find information about a person.
2 From the Look in list, select **InfoSpace Internet Directory Service**	To look for the person in InfoSpace Internet Directory Service.
3 In the Name box, enter your name	
4 Click **Find Now**	To begin the search.
Observe the message	It states whether the search results were successful. If the search results are successful you'll get a list of people with the same name and their e-mail addresses.
Observe the search results	
5 Click **Close**	To close the Find People dialog box.

Tell students to type their names in the Name box.

Tell students that the search results might not be successful.

Searching the Internet

Explanation

To search for information on the Internet, choose Start, Find, On the Internet. You can select a category for a search before starting. The categories that are available are:

- Find a Web page: You can select this category if you want to find a Web page that contains the information you're searching for.
- Find a person's address: You can select this option and find a person's mailing address or e-mail address.
- Find a business: You can select this option to find a business based on the type of business, and city and state where it is located.
- Previous searches: This category gives you a list of the searches you've made on various topics. The topics are listed as links. You can use these links to connect to the same topics again.
- Find a map: You can use this category to search for an address, place, or landmark.

Do it! **B-2: Searching the Internet**

Here's how	Here's why
1 Choose **Start**, **Find**, **On the Internet...**	To open Internet Explorer.
Observe the left pane	This pane consists of different categories that you can use for your search.
2 In the left pane, under Choose a category for your search, verify that **Find a Web page** is selected	Choose a category for your search: ⊙ **Find a Web page** ○ Find a person's address ○ Find a business ○ Previous searches ○ Find a map You'll find a Web page.
3 In the Find a Web page containing box, enter **Windows 98**	Find a Web page containing: Windows 98 Brought to you by MSN Search [Search] You'll search for information on Windows 98.
4 Click **Search**	(To display the search results.) You'll have to wait before you can see the search results in the left pane.
5 In the left pane, under Web Directory Sites, click **Windows 98 Tips & Tricks**	6. Windows98.org 7. Windows 98 Central 8. Windows Guide - Angela Lilleystone 9. Windows 98 Tips & Tricks (You'll need to scroll down.) To open the Web page in the right pane.
6 Scroll down and observe the Web page	You can click on any of these links for information.
7 Close Internet Explorer	

Working with Internet search tools

Explanation

You can find information on the Internet by using Internet search tools. Almost all Web sites have a *search engine*. A search engine is a program that searches for keywords in documents or databases on the World Wide Web, newsgroups, Gopher menus, and FTP archives. Usually search engines not only display related topics but also links to sites where you can find more information. The speed with which you gain access to the required information depends on the efficiency of the search engine of that Web site. Some of the most popular Web sites that provide search engines are Lycos, Excite, Yahoo!, Infoseek, and AOL NetFind.

To work with Internet search tools:

1 Open Internet Explorer.
2 In the Address box, enter the address of a Web site that provides a search utility.
3 Press Enter or click Go.
4 Enter the keyword or phrase on which you want to find information.
5 Click the required button to begin the search.

Do it!

B-3:   Working with Internet search tools

Here's how	Here's why
1 Open Internet Explorer	You'll work with Internet search tools.
2 In the Address box, enter **www.yahoo.com**	You'll open this site to search for information on a topic.
3 Press (↵ ENTER)	To connect to the site.
4 In the Search box, enter **Computers**	
	You'll use the Internet search tools to search for information on Computers.
5 Click **Search**	To begin the search.
Observe the window	The search results appear.
Close Internet Explorer	

Tell students that if the information they're looking for is not available, the search results might not be successful.

Tell students to scroll through the window and view the search results.

Unit Summary: Working on the Internet

Topic A   In this unit, you learned how to **add active content** to the desktop and how to set **custom update schedules** for it. You also learned how to **delete** active content from the desktop.

Topic B   Finally, you learned how to **find** a person using the Find People dialog box and how to work with **Internet search tools** to find information on a topic.

Independent practice activity

1   Add active content on **sports** to the desktop from the **Active Desktop gallery**.

2   Set a custom update schedule for every **3** days at **6:00 P.M.** for the active content.

3   Delete the active content from the desktop.

4   Find your details in **Yahoo! People Search**.

5   Search for information on topics related to **Business** in **www.yahoo.com**.

Unit 7

Internet utilities

Complete this unit, and you'll know how to:

A Create Web pages using FrontPage Express.

B Filter Internet content, set security levels and create an Internet profile.

Topic A: Creating Web pages with FrontPage Express

Explanation

FrontPage Express is a software application you can use to create Web pages. FrontPage Express provides a graphical user interface to design Web pages. It automatically creates the HTML code needed to display text or graphics. HTML (HyperText Markup Language) is a language used to create Web pages. You don't need any prior knowledge of HTML or any other Web designing language to create a Web page in FrontPage Express. This is because FrontPage Express creates the code by itself. Whatever you write or insert in the screen will be automatically converted to HTML code. You can easily create a Web page that contains text, graphics, and background images. You also can format text and add links to Web pages.

Inserting text and background images

Background colors and images provide a distinct look to a Web site, making it easily identifiable to users. To start FrontPage Express, choose Start, Programs, Internet Tools, FrontPage Express. When you start FrontPage Express, a new blank Web page is automatically opened. You can add text and background to it and then save the Web page.

Adding text or a background image to a Web page is fairly simple. It is done the same way you add text to a document in Notepad or WordPad.

To add a background image:

1 Choose Format, Background to open the Page Properties dialog box.
2 Verify that the Background tab is active.
3 Check Background Image.
4 Click Browse to open the Select Background Image dialog box.
5 Click Browse to find the image file you want to insert.
6 From the Look in list, select the necessary folder.
7 Select the file to be inserted.
8 Click OK.

After you add text and background to your Web page, you need to save it. To save your Web page choose File, Save As.

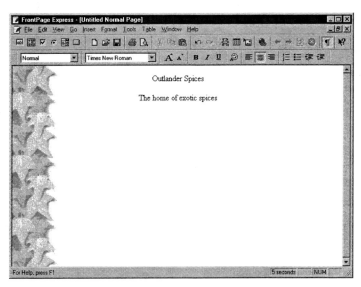

Exhibit 7-1: A Web page in the FrontPage Express window

Do it!

A-1:   Inserting text and background images

Here's how	Here's why
1 Choose **Start**, **Programs**, **Accessories**, **Internet Tools**, **FrontPage Express**	To open FrontPage Express. The FrontPage Express window looks similar to WordPad. The flashing insertion point indicates where the text will appear when you begin typing.
Maximize the window	
2 Type **Outlander Spices**	To add text to the Web page. This text will be the heading for the Web page.
3 Click	(The Center button is on the Format toolbar.) To center align the heading.
4 Press (↵ ENTER)	To move the insertion point to the next line.
5 Type **The home of exotic spices**	To add this text to the Web page.
6 Choose **Format**, **Background...**	To open the Page Properties dialog box. You'll insert a background image.
Verify that the **Background** tab is active	To view the Background tab options.
Observe the Background tab options	You can set a background image and change the color of the background and text. Notice that the Browse button isn't available.

7	Check **Background Image**	The Browse button is now available.
	Click **Browse**	To open the Select Background Image dialog box. You'll navigate to the image to be set as background.
8	Click **Browse**	
9	From the Look in list, select **StudentData**	You'll insert a file stored in the StudentData folder.
10	Select **Leaves**	To insert this file as the background.
	Click **Open**	
	Click **OK**	To close the dialog box and apply the background.
11	Choose **File**, **Save As...**	To open the Save As dialog box.
12	Edit the Page Title box to read **MyPage**	Page Title: MyPage
		To give a new name to the page.
	Click **As File**	(To open the Save As File dialog box.) You'll save the page as a file on your computer's hard disk and not on a Web site. It displays "Mypage" as the file name.
13	In the Save in list, verify that **StudentData** is selected	You'll save the file in this folder.
14	Click **Save**	
15	Choose **View**, **HTML...**	(To open the View or Edit HTML window.) To view the HTML code for Mypage. This is the code that FronPage Express creates for all that you did to the screen.
16	Click **OK**	

TIPS *Tell students that the file is saved as an .htm file.*

Formatting text

Explanation

You can format text by applying different fonts, changing colors, and sizes or by making text bold, italicized, or underlined. Formatting text in FrontPage Express is similar to formatting text in a word processor such as Microsoft Word. To make the text bold or italic, click the Bold or Italic button on the Format toolbar.

Do it!

A-2: Formatting text

Here's how	Here's why
1 Select **Outlander Spices**	You'll format this text.
2 Click [B]	(On the Format toolbar.) To make it bold.
3 From the Change Font list, select **Arial**	(On the Format toolbar.) To change the font to Arial.
4 Select **The home for exotic spices**	You'll format this text.
5 Click [I]	(On the Format toolbar.) To italicize the text.
6 Deselect the text	Click anywhere to deselect.
7 Click [save]	(The Save button is on the Standard toolbar.) To update the file.

Adding graphics to Web pages

Explanation

You can add images to your Web pages to illustrate products and ideas. For example, in the Web page of Outlander Spices, you can add pictures of spices and herbs. You also can insert the company logo on the Web page.

To add graphics to a Web page:

1   Choose Insert, Image to open the Image dialog box.
2   Verify that From File is selected.
3   Click Browse.
4   From the Look in list select the image file to be inserted.
5   Click Open.

Do it!

A-3: Adding graphics to Web pages

Here's how	Here's why
1 Place the insertion point after **Outlander Spices**	You'll insert the graphic below Outlander Spices.
2 Press ⟵ ENTER	
3 Choose **Insert**, **Image...**	(To open the Image dialog box.) You'll insert a graphic in the page.
4 Verify that **From File** is selected	
5 Click **Browse**	To locate the graphic to be inserted in the page.
6 From the Look in list, select **StudentData**	(If necessary.) To select an image from StudentData.
7 Select **Companylogo**	You'll insert this graphic.
8 Click **Open**	To insert the graphic.
Observe the page	The image appears on the page.
9 Update the file	Click the Save button on the Standard toolbar.

Adding links between Web pages

Explanation

You establish connections between Web pages by adding *hyperlinks*. A hyperlink is a word, phrase, image or symbol that is clicked to open another Web page. A hyperlink is usually underlined and has a different color than the rest of the document.

To add a link between two Web pages:

1 Place the insertion point at the location where you want the hyperlink.
2 Type the text that you want as the hyperlink.
3 Select the text you have typed for the hyperlink.
4 Choose Insert, Hyperlink to open the Create Hyperlink dialog box.
5 Click the World Wide Web tab.
6 From the Hyperlink Type list, select File.
7 In the URL box, type the location of the page you want to connect.
8 Click OK.

Do it!

A-4:   Adding links between Web pages

Here's how	Here's why
1 Place the insertion point as shown	*The home of exotic spices*
	You'll insert a hyperlink below this line.
Press (↵ ENTER)	
2 Type **Click here for more details**	
3 Select **Click here for more details**	This text will be the hyperlink to another page.
4 Choose **Insert, Hyperlink...**	To open the Create Hyperlink dialog box.
5 Click the **World Wide Web** tab	(If necessary.)
6 From the Hyperlink Type list, select **file:**	To create a hyperlink to another file.
7 Edit the URL as shown	URL: file://C:\StudentData\Products.html
	To specify the name of the file to which you'll link this page.
8 Click **OK**	To close the Create Hyperlink dialog box.
9 Deselect the text	
Observe the hyperlink	Notice that the text is underlined and blue.
Update the file	
10 Close FrontPage Express	

Viewing a local Web page

Explanation

To see how the Web pages you create in FrontPage Express actually look, you can view them in your browser. The Web pages might appear different in the browser. For example, the browser might not identify some fonts, and as a result the page might not appear properly. You should preview Web pages you've created on the browser so that you can make changes before making them available on the Internet. You also can check the hyperlinks you've created to see if they connect to the appropriate Web pages.

Do it!

A-5: Viewing a local Web page

Here's how	Here's why
1 Open Internet Explorer	(Click Start, Programs, Internet Explorer.)
2 Choose **File**, **Open...**	To display the Open dialog box.
3 Click **Browse**	To locate the page you want to open.
4 From the Look in list, select **StudentData**	
5 Select **mypage**	This is the file you'll open.
Click **Open**	
6 Click **OK**	To open the page in Internet Explorer.
Observe the page	The page that you created opens in Internet Explorer.
7 Click **Click here for more details**	To view the linked Web page.
8 Close Internet Explorer	

Topic B: Setting Internet properties

Explanation

Filtering Internet content ensures that unwanted sites aren't accessed. In addition, Internet Explorer also can set security levels. By setting the security level to High, you can ensure that information that can destroy the contents of your computer isn't downloaded. You also can create an Internet Profile so that you don't have to type your personal information every time to complete online forms.

Filtering Internet content

Windows 98 can filter unwanted Internet content. Most Internet sites have ratings based on their content. You can filter out content that contains varying levels of language, nudity, sex, and violence. If someone tries to open a site that has unwanted content, the operating system identifies the content and filters it to make the page unavailable for viewing.

To filter Internet content:

1 Open Internet Explorer.
2 Choose Tools, Internet Options to open the Internet Options dialog box.
3 Click the Content tab.
4 Click Enable to open the Content Advisor dialog box.
5 Make necessary changes in the settings.
6 Click OK.

Do it!

B-1: Filtering Internet content

Here's how	Here's why
1 Open Internet Explorer	You'll filter Internet contents.
2 Choose **Tools, Internet Options...**	To open the Internet Options dialog box.
3 Click the **Content** tab	To view the Content tab options.
4 Under Content Advisor, click **Enable**	To open the Content Advisor dialog box.
5 In the Select a category to view the rating levels list, verify that **Language** is selected	You'll view the rating levels for Language.
6 Drag the slider as shown	
Under Adjust the slider to specify what users are allowed to see, observe the levels	

7	Click the **Approved Sites** tab	To view its contents.
	Observe the contents of Approved Sites	You can list the approved and disapproved sites here.
8	Click **Cancel**	To close the Content Advisor dialog box.

Setting security levels

Explanation

By setting security levels for your computer, you can avoid downloading content that might be harmful to your computer's data. The security level can be set as High, Medium, Medium-low, and Low. Your computer is most secure when set to High. If you lower the security level, Internet Explorer prompts for verification before you can actually access a site.

The security levels are categorized into four zones. You can set security levels for the four different zones described in the following table.

Zone	Description
Internet	All Web sites that don't fall into the category of any other zone are assigned the Internet zone. The default security level for this zone is Medium.
Local intranet	All Web sites that form a part of your organization's intranet are included in this zone. The default security level for this zone is Medium-low.
Trusted sites	Web sites that can't possibly damage your computer's data are included in this zone. The default security level for this zone is Low.
Restricted sites	Web sites that can potentially damage the contents of your computer are included in this zone. The default security level for this zone is High.

To set security levels:

1 Open Internet Explorer.
2 Choose Tools, Internet Options.
3 Click the Security tab.
4 From the Select a Web content zone to specify its security settings list, select a zone.
5 Select the security level for the zone.
6 Click Apply.
7 Click OK.

Do it!

B-2: Setting security levels

Here's how	Here's why
1 Click the **Security** tab	To view the Security tab options.
2 From the Select a Web content zone to specify its security settings list, select **Restricted sites**	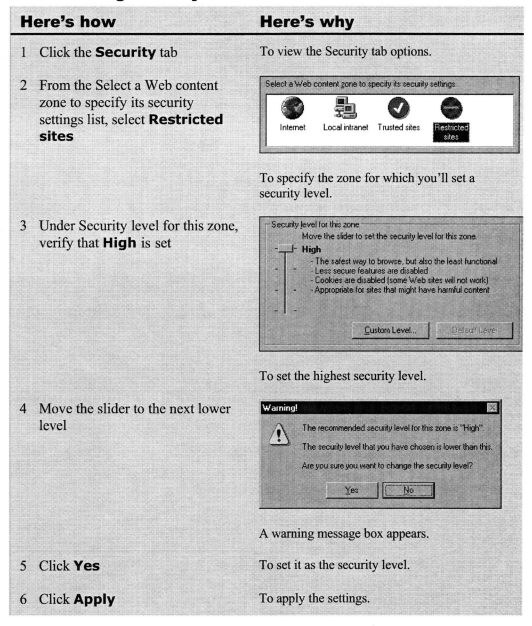
	To specify the zone for which you'll set a security level.
3 Under Security level for this zone, verify that **High** is set	
	To set the highest security level.
4 Move the slider to the next lower level	
	A warning message box appears.
5 Click **Yes**	To set it as the security level.
6 Click **Apply**	To apply the settings.

Creating an Internet profile

Explanation

An Internet profile usually contains personal data and information. After you create an Internet profile, you don't have to repeatedly type this information when filling out online forms. The profile information is reused whenever you access a Web page that requires you to enter your profile details. The profile information you set can be changed and updated as needed.

Before your personal information is submitted on a Web page, you receive an alert message. If the Web page you're sending information to isn't safe, Internet Explorer warns you before you send any information. A Web page is considered unsafe if others can view the information you send to it. After you receive the warning message, you can confirm whether you want to send the information to that Web page.

To create an Internet profile:

1 Open Internet Explorer.

2 Open the Internet Options dialog box.

3 Click the Content tab.

4 Under Personal Information, click My Profile.

5 Verify that Create a new entry in the Address Book to represent your profile is selected.

6 Click OK to open the Main Identity Properties dialog box (as shown in Exhibit 7-2).

7 Under Name, type your first, middle, and last name, nickname, and your e-mail address.

8 Click Add.

9 Click OK.

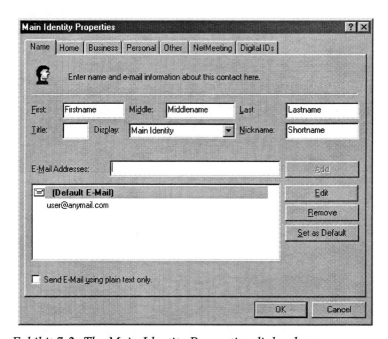

Exhibit 7-2: The Main Identity Properties dialog box

Do it!

B-3: Creating an Internet profile

Here's how	Here's why
1 Click the **Content** tab	To view the Content tab options.
2 Under Personal information, click **My Profile**	To open the Address Book - Choose Profile dialog box.
3 Verify that Create a new entry in the Address Book to represent your profile is selected	To make changes to the personal profile.
4 Click **OK**	To open the Main Identity Properties dialog box.
5 Verify that the Name tab is active	You'll enter information in this tab.
6 In the First box, enter your first name	To specify your first name.
In the Middle box, enter your middle name	To specify your middle name.
In the Last box, enter your last name	To specify your last name.
In the Nickname box, enter a nickname	To specify a nickname.
7 Edit the E-Mail Addresses box to read **yourfirstname@anymail.com**	To specify the e-mail address.
8 Click **Add**	To add the e-mail address to the E-Mail Addresses list.
9 Click **OK**	To confirm changes made to the profile.
10 Click **OK**	To apply the settings and close the dialog box.
Close Internet Explorer	

Tell students to enter their first names.

Unit Summary: Internet utilities

Topic A

In this unit, you learned how to create Web pages by using **FrontPage Express**. You learned how to insert text and background images on a Web page. You also learned how to format inserted text, add graphics and links to Web pages, and then view the local Web page.

Topic B

Finally, you learned how to set Internet properties by **filtering Internet content** to prohibit access to unwanted sites. You also learned how to **set security levels** as a precautionary measure to protect your computer from potential problems. Finally, you learned how to create an **Internet profile**.

Independent practice activity

1   Open FrontPage Express.

2   Enter the text **My Spice Store** in the Web page.

3   Change the font of the text to **Arial**.

4   On the next line, insert the image file **Spicepicture** from the StudentData folder.

5   In the next line, add the text **More Information** and set it as a hyperlink to the file **Information.html** in the StudentData folder.

6   Save the file by the name **myspice**.

7   View **myspice** in Internet Explorer.

8   Click the hyperlink to view the linked page.

9   Set the security level for restricted sites to **High**.

Windows 98: Advanced

Course summary

This summary contains information to help you bring the course to a successful conclusion. By using this information, you'll be able to:

A Use the summary text to reinforce what students have learned in class.

B Direct students to the next courses in this series (if any), and to any other resources that might help students continue to learn about Windows 98.

Topic A: Course summary

At the end of the class, use the following summary text to reinforce what students have learned. It is not intended as a script, but rather as a starting point.

Windows 98: Advanced

Unit 1

In this unit, students learned how to customize the Start menu. Students also learned how to **add** and **delete** items from the Start menu. Next, they learned how to **customize the taskbar** by adding shortcuts to the **Quick Launch toolbar** and adding the **Address** and **Links toolbars**. They also created a **floating toolbar**. Then, they learned how to set **custom folder options** to make changes in the appearance of a folder by choosing a background picture. They also learned how to **modify advanced folder settings** by changing the options in the Folder Options dialog box. Finally, they learned how to **assign a password** to a **screen saver**. Screen savers can be protected to avoid unauthorized use of personal documents.

Unit 2

In this unit, students learned how to view **file attributes** and **thumbnails**. File attributes are special properties of files and folders. The four types of file attributes are Read-only, Hidden, Archive, and System. They also learned how to enable thumbnails for graphic files. Then, they learned how to **hide** and **protect** data. They can hide a file or folder by checking the Hidden attribute for that file or folder. They can protect a file by converting it to a Read-only file. Finally, they learned how to view file extensions, view file associations in action, and modify file associations to open a file in a different application.

Unit 3

In this unit, students learned how to **add a printer** to their computers. They also learned how to set a **default printer**. Finally, they learned how to **manage the print queue** and set printer options.

Unit 4

In this unit, students learned how to launch a program using the **Run command** and **MS-DOS Prompt**. You can use these utilities when the program you want to run doesn't appear on the Start menu. Next, they learned how to delete unimportant files and recover hard disk space by using **Disk Cleanup, ScanDisk,** and the **Disk Defragmenter**. They learned to clean up the hard disk by using Disk Cleanup and detect and rectify hard disk errors by using ScanDisk. They also learned how to improve the speed of their computers by using the Disk Defragmenter. Finally, they used the **Scheduled Task Wizard** and the **Maintenance Wizard** to schedule tasks to be performed by their computers to improve their overall efficiency and for their maintenance.

Unit 5

In this unit, students learned how to use the **Windows 98 troubleshooters** to help troubleshoot printer and memory problems. They also learned how to use the **Getting Started Book** to search for help. Finally, they learned how to use the **Windows Update** utility to update their operating systems by downloading the updates that their computers require. They also learned how to use Support Information to view information on frequently asked questions.

Unit 6

In this unit, students learned how to **add active content** to the desktop and how to set **custom update schedules** for it. They also learned how to **delete** active content from the desktop. Finally, they learned how to **find** a person by using the Find People dialog box and work with **Internet search tools** to find information on a topic.

Unit 7

In this unit, students learned how to create Web pages by using **FrontPage Express**. They learned how to insert text and background images in a Web page. They also learned how to format inserted text, add graphics and links to Web pages, and then view a local Web page. They learned to set Internet properties by **filtering Internet content** to prohibit access to unwanted sites. They also learned how to **set security levels** as a precautionary measure to protect their computer from potential problems. Finally, they learned how to create an **Internet profile**.

Topic B: Continued learning after class

Point out to your students that it is impossible to learn how to effectively use any software in a single day. To get the most out of this class, it's important that students begin working with Windows 98 to perform real tasks as soon as possible. Course Technology also offers resources for continued learning.

Next courses in this series

This is the last course in the series.

Other resources

In addition to the other courses in this series, students might also find some of these Course Technology resources useful as they continue to learn about Windows 98. For more information, visit www.course.com.

- Microsoft Windows 98 Comprehensive Concepts and Techniques
  ISBN: 0-7895-4746-5
- Microsoft Windows 98-Illustrated Complete
  ISBN: 0-7600-5485-1
- Microsoft Windows 98-Illustrated ADVANCED
  ISBN: 0-7600-6084-3

Windows 98: Advanced

Quick reference

Button	Keystrokes	What It Does
Start	CTRL + ESC	Displays the Start menu
		Left aligns the text
		Center aligns the selected text
		Right aligns the text
B	CTRL + B	Makes the selected text bold
I	CTRL + I	Italicizes the selected text
	CTRL + S	Updates the active file
U	CTRL +U	Underlines the text

Index